Speaking of Florida

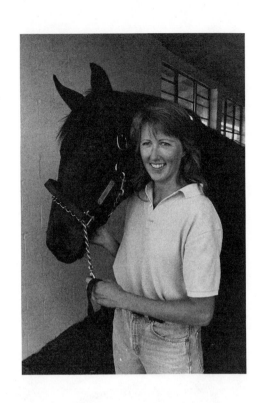

Photographs by Henry Rowland

and Walter Michot

Speaking
of Florida

William L. Pohl
and John Ames

University of North Florida Press / Jacksonville

Library of Congress Cataloging-in-Publication Data

Pohl, William L., 1955–
    Speaking of Florida / William L. Pohl and John Ames ;
photographs by Henry Rowland and Walter Michot
        p.   cm.
    ISBN 0-8130-1048-9
    1. Florida—Social life and customs. ˙ 2. Florida—
Biography.
3. Interviews—Florida.   I. Ames, John.   II. Title.
F316.P64   1991
975.9—dc20   90-21864

Half-title and title page photos: Ross Hooks and gator,
Michele Brennan and horse, Gene and Rusti Schuler and
chimp, all by Henry Rowland; William Foster by Walter
Michot.

The University of North Florida Press is a member of
University Presses of Florida, the scholarly publishing
agency of the State University System of Florida. Books
are selected for publication by faculty editorial commit-
tees at each of Florida's nine public universities: Florida
A&M University (Tallahassee), Florida Atlantic University
(Boca Raton), Florida International University (Miami),
Florida State University (Tallahassee), University of Central Florida (Orlando), University of Florida (Gainesville),
University of North Florida (Jacksonville), University
of South Florida (Tampa), University of West Florida
(Pensacola).
    Orders for books published by all member presses
should be addressed to University Presses of Florida,
15 NW 15th St., Gainesville, FL 32603.

Contents

Photo by Walter Michot

JOHN AMES

Introduction

FLORIDA IS BOTH THE nation's oldest and newest frontier. From the moment Ponce de Leon stepped ashore in 1513 to the moment of the most recent space launch, exploiters have meddled with the state, sometimes to its glory and sometimes to its shame. The people of Florida are of necessity adaptable up-and-comers, used to coping with change, but in recent years the pace of change has increased so much that in a few years, those who remember Florida in its numerous forms since the turn of the century will be gone, leaving little more than dry history and some views on vintage post cards. There will remain names, dates, and images aplenty, but how will we know anything of the human dimension of Florida's diverse population, as the state begins its sweeping metamorphosis? *Speaking of Florida* is an attempt to conserve a portion of something that cannot be made into a state park or put on the National Register of Historic Places: the personality of a people.

Change is nothing new in Florida. Its modern history began with the greatest and, in the minds of many, the worst change of all: the coming of the Europeans. Little is known of the Native American tribes in Florida at the moment Ponce de Leon stepped ashore. He reported a well-established culture, extending throughout the state and closely connected with a larger federation that covered the Southeast. Twenty years later, that culture lay in ruin, devastated by the impact of the newcomers.

This initial upheaval established the pattern of Florida's growth. Since the time of Ponce de Leon, native-born Floridians of many races and ethnic backgrounds have watched with wonder as their state has been invaded by outsiders drawn by Florida's special appeal as a place where dreams may come true. Though Ponce de Leon never found the Fountain of Youth, subsequent arrivals in Florida have continued to pursue dreams only slightly less fantastic, and in that pursuit have continually remade the state.

For three hundred years, Florida was the prize in many disputes involving the Spanish, the English, the French, the remaining Native Americans, and later the citizens of the newly created United States of America. Early maps reflect extensive change in the form of forts, missions, and settlements along the coasts, but far less change was seen in the interior. Easy access to Florida's coasts and the sheer extent of its coastline discouraged inland settlement. For most of Florida's history, there was always yet another place somewhere near the sea that was ripe for exploitation, and this situation formed the basis of one of the great paradoxes of Florida, one that continued well into the twentieth century. The state has endured exuberant development on its shores, while the interior of the state and its northern reaches have retained, by comparison at least, the character of an earlier time.

Over the years one grandiose design after another has been inflicted on Florida's coastline: the Castillo de San Marcos in St. Augustine, the Kennedy Space Center at Cape Canaveral, Miami Beach, the overseas railroad connecting the Keys, Davis Islands in Tampa—the list is long. And while these schemes, all reflecting the most up-to-date technology of their times, were being worked out by the seashore, Florida's interior and northern areas have remained a largely mysterious and far less developed area, serving as a refuge for those fleeing from the changes that were overwhelming the fringes of the state. Into the Everglades melted the remaining Seminoles, a tactic so effective that they were never dislodged. In another example of inland resistance, Florida was the last eastern state to abolish open-range cattle grazing, which hung on until 1949, when the Florida Fence Law was passed.

In the past, this "other Florida," as it has been called, has been a reassuring phenomenon for the state's lifelong residents, something solid and real when measured against the frequently trendy and often downright tacky coastal developments. For those familiar with the state as a whole, the existence of such a haven even made it possible to look with bemused affection on many of the tourist magnets to which Floridians have become so accustomed. In the past, they seemed simply an odd sidelight in a state that offered so much more to its inhabitants than its casual visitors saw. And for many years, even the increasing flow of new residents into Florida really seemed to pose no problem. They all appeared to want to live at the seaside, where change was familiar. Florida's coastlines were immense, and between the developments there were still stretches of relatively untouched shoreline, and always there were inland and northern Florida, aloof and dependable.

Then, in a startlingly short span of years, several factors combined to sweep the state into the most alarming rush of change in its history, a juggernaut of development that is threatening every corner of Florida, even its remotest areas.

First of all, the state's population has been quietly doubling every two decades since the turn of the century. By 1950, it had reached 2,770,000; by 1970, 6,791,400; by 1990, 12,797,300. Florida is already the fourth most populated state in the nation, and if this doubling phenomenon occurs again, it may well top the list in 2010. Today, Florida's coastlines are strained to the breaking point. The stretches of undeveloped beaches that existed even into the early seventies are gone, replaced by a nearly unbroken strip city. Only the northwestern coast of Florida above Crystal River has been spared, and even there evidences of development are beginning to surface.

At about the same time that the state's population hit a critical point, conditions improved for the remaking of long-neglected central Florida. In 1964 Interstate 75 opened up as the primary auto route into Florida and connected at Wildwood with the recently completed Florida Turnpike, a superhighway originating in Miami. This system, together with Interstate 4 cutting across the state from Tampa to Daytona Beach, opened up the center of Florida to exploitation, providing developers with core roadways around which to orient projects.

Then, in 1971, Disney World opened in Orlando, the heart of Florida's citrus belt. Within a few years, a county that had previously had little tourist appeal became the world's most attractive vacation destination. When Disney World was completed, there were about 5,500 hotel and motel rooms in Orange County. Presently, there are more than 40,000. Disney World and its satellite attractions, made easily accessible by I-75, the Florida Turnpike, and I-4, have sparked a flurry of development that has spread outward into central Florida, drastically changing its previously agrarian character.

Florida's improved transportation system, good weather, and attractive business climate have in the past twenty years drawn corporate operations in ever-increasing numbers; and where there are jobs, people follow. Every day nearly a thousand immigrants arrive in Florida, and this cascade of newcomers cannot all locate in Miami Beach (however much they might like to), so developers have turned their eyes elsewhere. The phrase "North Florida has been discovered" is now in vogue.

Rampant growth has lately taken its place among the greatest of public fears in a state that has placidly witnessed odd changes for the last 500 years. But change is no longer something about which residents make rueful jokes, secure in the knowledge that it will be conveniently restricted to the fringes. It's finally everywhere, and what's left of Florida's past is fading fast. One response to this predicament was the 1985 Growth Management Act, an attempt by the state legislature to bring some logic to the state's chaotic evolution.

The Growth Management Act and other measures like it may finally preserve something of Florida's physical past, but a more elusive element is being lost, and that is the personality of its population. In the next few years, Florida will undergo a makeover exceeded in dimension only by the initial decimation of its Native American population. Soon the present mixture of the state's peoples will be largely gone, lost in a flood of immigration.

William Pohl and Walter Michot, the originators of *Speaking of*

Florida, began the book as an act of what Pohl calls "cultural conservation." In its pages can be found a taste of the personality of a state on the verge of either annihilation or rebirth, depending on one's point of view, for in modern memory Florida's story has been in large part the story of those who are already here reacting to the changes brought on by those who continually arrive. Sometimes that reaction is delight, sometimes dismay. In recent years it has most often been outrage. For longtime residents, modern Florida is Paradise lost. For those arriving, it is Paradise gained. *Speaking of Florida* divides its pages evenly between both types. In their remarks, the character of the state's people and what Florida means to them is revealed, often in unexpected ways.

Many immigrants to Florida, for example, are far more interested in discussing their occupations or avocations than their adopted state. For them, Florida is primarily a backdrop against which they pursue their passions. Such people are reminders that Florida has always provided a home for individualists, but, though they say little directly about their surroundings, something of Florida's distinctiveness can be found between the lines. Melvin Fisher's exploits as a treasure hunter evoke Florida's connection with the Spanish Empire, as well as the role which the state's dangerous reefs have played in its maritime history. Fred Knoller, the world's oldest active bicycle racer, has chosen Florida as both a place to retire and a place to train for his sport, reflecting in his unique way two of Florida's most characteristic functions. Blimp pilot Jim Maloney, bandmaster William P. Foster, and others like them have pursued their individual dreams in Florida, contributing to its vitality.

Many natives of the state offer more direct insights on the nature of Florida, because their lives are so tightly woven into its fabric. Janetta Giles Norman tells of her childhood in a racially segregated Jacksonville and reminds us that the paradise pictured on Florida postcards of the period was largely a whites-only paradise, and her comments about drug dealing in her present-day neighborhood remind us that a legacy of discrimination still haunts the state. Thelma Cruce's tale of growing up in the backwoods of northern Florida evokes the spirit of its Cracker settlers. Henry C. Aparicio's reminiscences of his life in Ybor City call to mind the ethnic diversity that has been a continuing trademark of the state. Citrus grower Dorothy Conner Shipes and sponge museum operator Theofani Koulianos are other examples of Florida natives whose life experiences offer clear footnotes to the state's history.

Among the most interesting and instructive of the interview subjects are those—some natives and some transplants—who find Florida itself a phenomenon of intense interest. For them, the state is not just the place where they've come to pursue a dream, or the place where they've been raised; rather, it is a place of fascinating, almost magical attributes. Perhaps the most representative of these is film star Burt Reynolds, whose passion for Florida is both surprising and touching in a man who would be a celebrated citizen nearly anywhere he chose to live. Yet he remains devoted to Florida, recalling with relish his days as a barefoot schoolboy in the 1940s. For people like Reynolds, hotel owner Marcia Rogers, airboat enthusiast George Mercer, and poet Edmund Skellings, the state itself or some part of it has special meaning and is a subject they eagerly discuss, each articulating in his or her own way a very real but unquantifiable factor in Florida's growth: its mystique.

Like the multifaceted culture of which they are a part, the people in *Speaking of Florida* reveal themselves in a variety of ways. Sometimes reserved, sometimes aggressive, sometimes subtle, sometimes direct, sometimes tasteful, sometimes crass. Our primary concern in shaping their words was to retain a strong sense of their spoken expression, so we altered their grammar and syntax as little as possible, only doing so in the interests of clarity. Their remarks are presented as unbroken monologues, the style that we believe most effectively conveys their personalities.

Our most extensive work was done in ordering and abridging subjects' remarks, a process we began by transcribing our audiotapes onto computer disks. We then reordered the material for greatest coherence, since the original conversations had developed organically and had seldom considered first things first. The next step was to eliminate comments that did not directly contribute to the main theme of the interviews. Finally, we provided short transitions and clarifying phrases where necessary.

Once we had finished editing the interviews, we returned them to the subjects for their review. Corrections were restricted to matters of fact and opinion; subjects were not allowed the liberty of rephrasing or extensively expanding their remarks, a process we felt would have destroyed the sense of spontaneity in the interviews.

Many more interviews were done than were actually used. In making our final choices, we tried to balance gender, ethnic background, and geographical location. In addition, we wanted to provide insights into Florida's cultural development over the broadest possible span of time, from early in the century to the current day. We have presented the subjects in two sections, the first devoted to lifelong Floridians and the second to transplants.

What has emerged is a diverse sampling of Florida's human resources. Poised together on the brink of tremendous change, the people in *Speaking of Florida*—from the most venerable native to the newest immigrant—are linked by a common conviction that they are in the right place to pursue a dream. Though some of their dreams may ultimately prove to be Florida's undoing, their words provide some reassurance in the face of the stupefying statistics of growth, reminding us that the reality behind the numbers is not merely cold and mathematical but warm and human.

Photo by Walter Michot

PART ONE

*"Florida is my
natural home."*

Photo by Henry Rowland

Thelma Cruce

IN A STATE SOMETIMES CALLED America's playground, Thelma Cruce was raised in poverty and has lived a life of hard work. She is one of a vanishing breed of authentic Florida Crackers, tough-minded country people with a pioneer attitude. Until she was twenty-seven years old, she lived in a remote area of the North Florida backwoods. The nearest neighbors were four miles away. She never went to school and never saw a town until she was a young adult. Her only contact with the wider world was a sawmill settlement where she and her mother went to trade. They were usually paid in "babbitt," a currency issued by the mill for use at the company store. "I seen mighty few people from the outside," she says.

Her father was home only one night a week. He was engaged in a mysterious occupation about which she refuses to speculate. "He *said* he cut cordwood," she recalls doubtfully. He was a bad customer who once bit off a man's ear in a brawl and wouldn't hesitate to come after you with a gun. "When *he* come in the front door, *I* went out the back," she says with a shiver in her voice. He provided little toward the family's support and from early childhood the threat of starvation was familiar. In the winter, when there was nothing to be had from

Photo by Walter Michot

the garden, they would forage in the woods, sometimes uprooting palmettos for food.

When Thelma Cruce was married, her trousseau consisted of one pair of overalls and one dress. Her life improved when she rescued a stranded range cow and its calf. She reported it to the owners, but they allowed her to keep the animals. The calf grew up and was broken into an extremely useful and sweet-tempered ox. He enabled her to make a weekly trip with her children to the nearest town for supplies. "There in the city of Perry," she remembers, "weren't nothing but a courthouse, a store here and a store there and a store there." Even so, she says she had to learn how to act in such a big place. The fourteen-hour round trip became a highlight of the week and broadened her horizons.

In 1937, Cruce moved her family to the fringes of Gainesville. Life was still hard but better than it had been. Instead of trapping animals and collecting wild fruits for extra money, she broke horses, cleaned houses, and took in washing. Her husband sharecropped and occasionally sanded floors. All of her ten children were delivered at home. The last was born in 1954. By this time she was forty-four and had been working at a crate mill for six years. She continued at this low-paying job for twenty-three years, sometimes being called "Dummy" because of her background. She says, "I'd laugh at 'em. Nothing made me mad. In a way it made me feel good, 'cause I knowed I was dumb, but I knowed more'n they did." In 1971, she was treated unfairly at the mill and quit.

Since that time she has managed laundromats, an occupation that includes mopping, scrubbing, and washing clothes by the pound. In 1982, she was near death as the result of a ruptured appendix, and can remember lying on the operating table and hearing the doctor say she wouldn't make it. Cruce dismissed this remark. She had no intention of dying and was back at work in a few weeks. The doctor wanted to know what she was raised on that had made her so tough. After nearly eight decades of hard labor, she says she's as weak now as she was strong in her youth, but she still puts in six days a week at the laundromat.

In spite of having had to scratch for a living in Florida, Cruce is loyal to her home state. "There was a lady in the laundromat complaining about how the ones up north had TV's in 'em and were so much nicer. She says to me, 'I thought Florida was supposed to be like heaven,' I told her, 'If you're looking for a seat in heaven, you're highly mistaken. This ain't it. I wouldn't come into your home and complain. If you want to complain, git a ticket up north.' Florida is my natural home, and I come so far from how I was raised, it's a miracle."

"I WAS BORN IN 1910 and raised up in Taylor County, twelve miles on the other side of Perry, Florida. Ain't nothing out there now but woods. I don't even know where it's at myself, hardly, when I go through there. My mama never had a stove. She cooked on a hearth fire or outside. If we was short of rations, I'd go out and gather some wild mustard weed, some pepper grass (not too much—it's strong), and some potato leaves from the garden. That made a delicious pot of greens. At least it was then. I don't know how it would taste now.

"Never went to school a day in my life, but my mother had a fourth-grade education and she made me say my ABCs forwards and backwards a hundred times before I went to sleep at night. I can read the newspaper and git a lot out of it. Course, there's some big words I don't understand, but I jest skip 'em and go right on.

"My father didn't never come home only Saturdays. Jest once a week. Nobody knowed where he was the rest of the time. He never did support us. We had to git it from scratch. As fur as that, me and Mother'd walk three and four miles—weed fence, pick cotton, gather chufers. That's something you don't know anything about, I don't imagine. They're a little old hard nut thing, and they jest grow in clusters. People used to plant 'em fer their hogs. We'd grub them up and beat 'em off. And we'd break corn, jest like the men did. Course I'd been a-doin' it all my life, but me and mother jest naturally went on the job when I was about eight years old.

"At home, me and mother had a little place to plant. I'd go down it with a club axe and cut the little roots in streaks and we'd grub it up and break them roots out. Then I'd pull the plow and she'd plow me. I started doing that when I was about ten years old. She wanted to do it, but she didn't weigh but ninety-five pounds. I felt like I was more mannish than she was. I always put myself to do better! We'd have two rows of mustard greens and two of collard. And we'd have a couple rows of sweet potatoes and about four, five rows of corn, and a hill of squashes round and about and eggplant round and about. We had our food like that, and I had a little white dog. We called him Snowball. I'd take that axe on Saturday morning and Sunday morning, and I taken Snowball—he was a rabbit dog; I mean he didn't fail—and I'd go out and I'd catch ten or fifteen rabbits and dress 'em. Then me and my mother'd walk eight miles to black quarters and sell 'em fifteen cent apiece to git us some extrys.

"My daddy'd come home on Saturday. He'd bring fifty cent worth of meal, quarter's worth of lard, fifty cent in money and a old pouch of snuff (that's the reason I hate it so much) fer my mother, and a red apple and a piece of peppermint candy. Well, I did not git any of that candy and apple. My daddy seen that my mother eat all of that. And I said, 'Well, if I live to be a grown woman, anybody give me a piece of peppermint candy or a red apple, I'm gonna chunk it at 'em.' And I never been bothered with it.

"So, when I got, I reckon, about twelve years old, I was cutting crossties. My brother'd come home, and he'd help me saw down cypress trees. I'm scared of a falling tree, but once they was on the ground, I done it all. Well, sometimes my mother helped me saw 'em up. I'd go down the side of them things and score-hack 'em, you see. You don't know what that is, but you'd take a club axe and score-hack 'em about that far apart, all the way down—jest so deep. Then you'd take this broad axe that's got a smooth side to it and hew that thing into shape, jest as smooth as you like. Hew it off and then saw it up into lengths. I could hew 'em near about looked like you'd sawed 'em. Course, I was used to it: knowed how to throw that axe.

"When the crossties give out we still had to do something and there was a feller, I think his name was Mitchell, Steve Mitchell. He had a turpentine still. I chipped turpentine. Not very long, but I did chip turpentine. You cut the bark in a 'V.' The turpentine would come down that and drip into a cup down here, fastened on the bottom of the tree. Once ever' other week, we went back with a scoop and a bucket. We dipped that turp and put it in the bucket. My right leg would git plumb stiff from toting that bucket on one side. I'd tote it from about as fur as here to the road out yonder and pour it in a big barrel. They had big barrels, like the dumpsters around here but it was big barrels. You'd dip so fur with turpentine, then you'd pour it in that barrel and take another route. That didn't last too long, but we always found something else to do when a job run out.

"One thing me and my brother done was catch alligators and skin 'em. A gator has caves jest like a gopher, you know, only they're in ponds. We'd watch 'em in the water and we could see when they'd go to the caves. And then we'd find 'em and joog a stick down there and we could feel him. Then we'd know where to staub him so he couldn't git out. If you drive sticks down over the cave where they can't git out and git air, they'll drown. All you got to do is go pull him on out the next morning and skin him. Some of 'em we had to hook. We'd get a pole about twenty foot long with a iron hook on the end of it and run it in there. He'd be ornery and fighting with something goin' down in on him and he'd snap it. Sometimes it took me and my brother both to pull 'em out, but mostly I'd pull 'em out and he'd stand at the cave and chop his head open or shoot him when he came out. We have caught gators that would be eight or nine foot long. One time we had a gator hooked in the bottom jaw under his tongue and he couldn't git it out. So we pulled, and we got part of his nose out. From their eyes to the end of their nose tells you how many feet long the gator is. You jest count one foot for each inch of their nose. This one was nine foot long and he was a-fighting. Buddy, he fought! My brother had to git around to shoot him, so I had to handle him by myself, but the further out of the cave he come, the wider he'd open his mouth. I was beginning to look a way down in yonder. That's a scary look, down the throat of a nine-foot alligator. Them old teeth, you know. He had terrible teeth! I was a-hollering to my brother, I said, 'I'm a-gonna turn him loose!' He said, 'You turn loose—he'll catch you!' I said, 'Well, I cain't take this!' but I kept on pulling. Whenever my brother'd see I was fixing to turn him loose, he'd holler, 'If you do, he'll catch you,' and that give me courage to— well, it weren't courage, it were jest fear. Seem like to me the gator was gitting closer to me but he weren't 'cause I kept running backwards holding a tight line on him. We finally got him out, and my brother shot him—killed him. We'd git five dollars fer a hide like that. Today you'd git a hundred.

"I got married but the work didn't git no lighter. I didn't know what marrying was fer. I really didn't, 'cause back in them days elder people didn't talk to younger people—the facts of life. I was jest plumb dumb. I didn't know nothing. My brother and sister-in-law was the cause of it, 'cause it was in '28 and it was hard, panic times. They kept on saying, 'If she marries him, she'll have a provider,' and he said, 'If she marries me, she won't want fer nothing.' Well, that's true, but I've wanted fer *something* a lotta times. We got married that morning at nine o'clock. We went back home and I plowed right by his side until the crop was made. Next morning, got up and plowed till twelve. Then him and his mother went to peddling, selling milk and butter and stuff like that to git a little money. I stayed there and done the wash and ironing and mopped the floors. That's all I knowed. It didn't bother me one bit in the world. I thought I had to go through with all that.

"After me and my husband was married, we really hit it hard, 'cause between one baby and another was times I couldn't git out and make my part of it. It was jest him and he was, well, like he is now. He don't provide. He don't know nothing in the world about providing fer anybody at all. But I never did think nothing about it. I never did look down on him fer not doing that. I was used to it. My daddy was like that, you see. It was jest go ahead Thelma and do it, and I jest went ahead and kept everything a-going. I went to bed many a night a-crying, 'Where's my other mouthfuls gonna come from to feed my children?' The next morning I'd git up and I'd be setting there and I'd look out and see that old chicken walking across the yard and I'd go out there and git him and wring his neck and make a big old pot of meal soup. We had a good dinner. Cook some greens. It weren't fancy but we had something to eat. We weren't out there stealing, knocking and a-framming people like they are these days. That's the reason I feel like they can do it if they want to—they can. I done it. I washed fer my husband's sister-in-law fer fifty cent a week. Course, fifty cent in them days would go as fur as five dollars now. Then it was fifty cent a week to mop and clean her house. That was a dollar a week. That holp a long ways.

"I say my favorite ox raised my first five children, because he pulled the plow and made corn to feed us. He was a sweet-natured animal. You didn't have to holler and beat and fram and jerk him around. You'd jest plow straight and when he'd git to the end of the row, he'd jest turn around and stop where he belonged on the other side. He always minded. Pulled the wagon into town. If he didn't raise my children, he sure holp a whole lot.

"We come over here to Gainesville in '37, and we put out two farms sharecropping. Course, when you sharecrop, the other fella gits the share and you git the work. It was with my husband's brother, and he taken everything out of our house. He made us live, me and my husband and four children, off a dollar and a quarter a week. When my baby was born in '40, they wouldn't even carry me to the doctor. They was told, but they said, 'We can't come.' And I lived about as fur as from here to yonder—that building over there—to their house. I delivered that baby myself and done everything right on. My doctor bills fer my children, all of the ten—I believe I'm telling the truth, I don't believe I'm lying—I bet all ten of 'em didn't cost me fifty dollars. Every one born at home. I was out at work, doing the washing and everything else, by the time they was a month old. Nothing never did stop me.

"I worked at Adkin's Crate Mill from '48 to '71. Started off at forty-five cent an hour. I drug down and graded cleats. I did that till my boss man had a heart attack and they put me under another man, and I told 'em, 'You put me under him, I'm gone.' And so they put me under him. What I was doing, I was laying cleats on two chains, you know, where they make the boxes. Well, he taken me off there and put two black girls up there, one on each side, and put me back there a-lifting and putting up stock. Big old bundles of boxes behind four machines. I reached up and got my purse and walked out. I been operating laundromats ever since.

"I got in the habit of keeping busy. I'm a-doing something about all the time till I git so sleepy I fall asleep. Course, I'm going on seventy-nine, and I'm a-thinking about trying to change and, you know, taking a little slow-up, but it might not work. I might not do it."

—Interview by John Ames

Henry Cobb

EVEN WHEN FLORIDA WAS a virtual wilderness, the mail got through—
by packet boats, postmen on horseback, and trains. Along coastal re-
gions there were even "barefoot mailmen" who slung mail satchels
and shoes over their shoulders and traversed the beaches on foot.

There was also Henry Cobb. In 1938 he bought a Model-A Ford,
used, for $200. In 1940, he landed a job with the U.S. Postal Service.
Over his forty-two-year career Cobb and the car faithfully made his
appointed rounds along the rural Bunnell Star Route. The two were
so long-lived, they became known personally by almost everyone all
the way down to Flagler.

Neither rain nor winds, rust nor time have stopped man or car very
long. They're getting some age on them, but nothing serious that
can't be fixed. When things go wrong with the car, Cobb consults a
weathered, dog-eared, 1931 Ford owner's handbook, yellowed with
age. He keeps a small inventory of spare parts in the attic of his house.
A shade tree mechanic, he uses pulleys attached to an old live oak
in the back yard to hoist the car's engine every 100,000 miles for re-
building. More than 700,000 miles later, the car and its owner are
still running strong.

Photo by Walter Michot

"I CAME TO FLORIDA from Alabama with my parents one year after I was born in 1916. My Dad worked for the Florida East Coast Railroad pumping water out of Lake Windermere at the Neoga Pump Station. We fed the water to the steam engines. We moved all up and down the Florida coast with the railroad until I married and set myself up here in Bunnell.

"In 1940 I started delivering mail on the Bunnell Star Route. I didn't quit until 1982, although around 1944 I moonlighted as a projectionist at the Bunnell picture show. Stuck with that for a little while. Maybe twenty years.

"I always grew up around Model-A Fords. They first come out in 1928. My Dad got one. In 1938 I bought the flivver I have now for two hundred dollars, used. It was seven years old and probably already had a hundred thousand miles on it. I've gone through six engines and put on another six hundred thousand miles. I still get twenty miles to the gallon. Always used super premium except during the war, when we had ration cards like this one in my wallet here. We used anything we could get a hold of, like kerosene.

"In 1955 I took a Model-A and made it into a skeeter. Took off the body and stuck on a seat and windshield. I had a dirt box on the back and used it to haul around junk. You get to know the cars growin' up around 'em. I'm what you might call a shade tree mechanic. When something breaks I get into it, figure it out, and fix it under a shade tree in the backyard. I learned most of what I know just from common sense.

"Every time a part wore out on the Model-A, I replaced it. I'm a perfectionist. Keep spare parts in my attic and a spare engine, along with a muffler, door handles, running board matting, and a water pump. When it'd come time to change the engine I'd overhaul it, grind valves, and work on the rear end. All them kinds of doings, but only after the mail round was done on Saturday, of course.

"When I first took the Star Route out of Bunnell it was a twenty-five and eight-tenths of a mile route. It had about twenty mailboxes. I knew everyone. It was a contractor job and you had to furnish your own car, so I used my Model-A. Over the years they kept adding more houses and mailboxes. By the time I quit in 1982, the route was a forty-six and one-tenth mile haul and it had some two hundred mailboxes. The place is getting built up some.

Henry Cobb   13

"It never occurred to me to give up the old Lizzie. The Model-A is the perfect car to do the job. It's only about four feet across so there's no problem reachin' over to deliver mail to boxes on the right side of the road. You don't have to keep sliding on the seat like you would with the wider modern cars. My car is almost six feet high, so I can keep up to six sacks of mail in the back seat. And it idles low—barely a hum—so it gets better mileage than most modern cars its size.

"Oh, I've modernized the car some. Put in a CB radio. I'm known as 'Model-A Mailman'—that's my code name, oddly enough. Also got me an AM-FM stereo radio inside and a new horn right next to the old one. I had to put on turn signal lights when that became the law. I also put on wider seventeen-inch tires.

"I still have to choke the engine by hand in the mornings, but I also have an electric starter. Pull down the hand throttle to get some gas primed in there and push the button. It don't exactly roar to life but eventually it gets to purring. In case of a breakdown, I have a hand crank which doubles as a lug wrench. I also carry a hand air pump for my tires.

"I almost never missed a round in forty-two years. I recall driving in hurricanes to get the mail through. Once I was along A1A near Flagler Beach to get to five mailboxes. The waves and ocean would be level along the road. Foam was scudding ahead and the palms was all bent back. I'd push on until the water flooded seventeen inches above its normal level. That's the height of my updraft carburetor. If it got wet the car would conk out. I wore a slicker in those blows and was always on the lookout for fallen electric lines and downed trees. Today they close the roads, but back then they didn't.

"My car is fast. Top speed is still around sixty-five miles an hour, downhill. I can go fifty on the straightaways. I have a flying quail on my radiator cap. That was the sign of a fast getaway car in the gangster movies.

"I've lived through several postmasters. One offered me a jeep but I turned it down. No good reason to change. I reckon I'll stick with the Model-A the rest of my life."

—*Interview by William Pohl*

Henry C. Aparicio

IN AN AGE WHEN the Hispanic influence in Florida has grown to such a degree that the state has nervously mandated English as its official language, it is ironic that Henry C. Aparicio spends so much of his time trying to keep alive the memory of Ybor City, Tampa's celebrated ethnic quarter. He can be found at least once a week at the Ybor City State Museum, serving as an oral historian. In a sense, his living presence among the tastefully arranged photographs and displays capsulizes the difference between Ybor City's present and its past, sometimes called *la edad de oro,* the golden age. Today, it is an area of restored buildings, most of which used to be something else. The beautiful brick cigar factories that were the reason for Ybor City's founding in 1886 have become shopping malls full of boutiques and restaurants. Seventh Avenue, the area's main street, is arched by colorful lights and kept free of litter but is largely empty. Certainly it is a far cry from the scene described in museum literature by historian Tony Pizzo: "The bubbling mass of promenaders with admiring eyes and Latin smiles afforded a most delicious experience." The sad fact is that changing times and urban renewal have left the ethnic community in Tampa with no real physical center, but

its spiritual heart still remains accessible through the warm remembrances of people like Henry C. Aparicio, whose father was among the greatest "Princes of the Factories."

Manuel Aparicio was not, as might be expected from his unofficial title, an industrialist. Rather, he was one of an elite corps of *lectores,* highly paid men whose profession was to read to the *tobaqueros* as they rolled the cigars that made Tampa famous. These readers occupied a position of unique prestige and influence in the Latin community. As members of a lector's family, Henry Aparicio, his mother, Milagro, his two sisters, Mary and Louisa, and his brother, Manuel, enjoyed a reflected glory. Though Aparicio has had a productive career of his own as a teacher of drafting and practical geometry, he seems most content when passing along recollections of his accomplished father. Then again, he is a man who enjoys preserving things, as evidenced by the satisfaction with which he points out his sporty 1967 Camaro. Aparicio himself is remarkably well preserved, despite his seventy-three years, and he continues to do his part in keeping alive memories of the singular culture into which he was born.

"I WAS VERY PROUD to be the child of a lector. It was like having a movie star as a parent. Everywhere we went in the community, he was recognized and people were always coming up to ask him something. He looked the part, too. He was six feet tall, broad-shouldered. Kept himself in good condition by doing calesthenics in the yard. I would say he was very aware of his appearance. I couldn't count the number of suits he had. Of course, he was an actor, too. He put on shows—acted and directed—at all the *centros,* the ethnic clubs in Ybor City and West Tampa, but this was just—what do you call it?—oh, yes, 'moonlighting' from his profession as a reader. Manuel Aparicio was the best of all the lectores, and I'm not saying that because he was my father. Many people told me the same thing. One man said, 'You know, I got a college education listening to your father.'

"You have to understand that the men who came to work in the cigar factories were from metropolitan areas, and there was nothing here when they arrived. Tampa didn't make Ybor City, Ybor City made Tampa. In 1886 there were just a few hundred people here, and the city only took off after the cigar industry came. So the workers had to import their own cultural opportunities. They had a great hunger for information and learning, but they couldn't go to school because they had to work all day. And they started very young. You see this chair I'm sitting on? It has those little blocks under the feet to make it taller because a child worked in it. This was why they employed a lector. Let's put it this way, instead of the pupils going to the teacher, the teacher came to the pupils.

"And his role in the community was that of a scholar. For example, people would ask him all the time to write letters for them. They would tell him what they wanted to say and he would write it down. Of course, he would change it around. That's what they wanted him to do. They had the feelings but they didn't have the words. A man might want to tell his mother he loved her, but just saying 'I love you' wasn't enough. My father could word it so that the man's mother cried. And he wrote a beautiful hand, so the letters were real treasures for whoever received them. It was a matter of great prestige for any family to invite the family of the reader to dinner. They were such knowledgeable men and such good storytellers. You must remember that at this time there was no radio and no television. That was the only entertainment they had, a reader coming to the house to visit. They were treated as real celebrities. Even when my father sat on his own porch with his family, a crowd, especially children, would gather to listen to him tell stories. It was considered a normal thing.

"My father first came to Ybor City from Madrid, Spain, to visit an uncle, and he saw a reader at work. He was only eighteen, but he had been attending the University of Madrid, and was a brilliant man. He spoke several languages—most of the readers were at least trilingual. My father could take a newspaper in, let's say, English and translate it into Spanish as he read, and you'd never know he wasn't reading the original in Spanish. So, when he saw that reader at work, he said to himself, 'I can do this.' He practiced and interviewed at different factories, and then they voted to see if he would be hired.

"This whole thing of the readers was run strictly by the workers. Management didn't like it. They wanted to keep the workers as ignorant as possible, and they accused the readers of being instigators, but I don't believe they were. My father didn't say, 'I'm gonna read this and that.' The workers had the Committee Lector, the reader's committee, and that committee chose what he read. It could be Shakespeare or Don Quixote or stories that were like soap operas, continued from one day to the next. The committee also collected the money from the workers to pay the lector. Each worker gave something like twenty-five cents a week. In a factory with five hundred workers, that would come to five or six times what the workers made, but they were glad to give it—they craved knowledge that much.

"So they hired my father. He became famous for his characterization. He would make up a voice for all of the characters in the reading, one for Juan, one for Maria. If there was an old man or an old lady—or if there was a German, he'd give him a German accent. If you couldn't see him up there on his stand, or if he came into the back of the room or something, you'd swear there was a German back there, it was so different from his usual voice! He made up all those voices and then he kept track of which was which. It wasn't just reading. He made it a drama. All the lectores were actors, but it was done with the voice alone. And you had to make yourself heard. There was nothing to amplify the sound. It was funny. I remember I could always tell when my father was going to work because he would gargle with honey and lemon juice. When I heard him gargle, I knew it was time for work.

"The regular workers started at six A.M., but the lector didn't go in until ten. He read until noon. In the morning, it was usually the news and other types of information. Everything from what's new in fashion to the latest in medicine. Many of the cigar workers couldn't even read, but they could talk about so many things—painting, literature—because they heard about them through the lector. His way of presenting it made them interested. Lectores really were teachers.

"At noon the factories got really hot, so the lector would leave and come back at two and read until four. In the afternoon it was mostly stories. The most popular were those soap operas I mentioned before. My father would read up to some place where the characters were in trouble and then close the book and say, 'To be continued tomorrow.' I myself used to run over to the factory after school to learn what happened to Juan or Maria. Housewives would come out of the houses near the factory with their parasols and their knitting and sit by the windows listening to the soap operas. Men used to come to the house after work and beg my mother to tell them what was going to happen the next day. 'Please, Mrs. Aparicio. We won't be able to sleep if we don't know.' She'd say, 'Believe me, I'd like to know as much as you!' If the family asked him, he would just say, 'Wait until tomorrow.' Sometimes, if we were lucky, we would know because we'd hear him practicing. Having the soap operas in the afternoon actually cut down on absenteeism, because bachelors might finish their quota of cigars in the morning, and they wouldn't need as much money as the family men, but they would come back to the factory anyway so they wouldn't miss any of the story.

"When the lector was reading, there must be absolute silence. I'll tell you how heavy the rule was. One time my father was working in this factory over in West Tampa, Garcia y Vega, and the owner of the factory had some friends or tourists come in while he was reading. The owner was taking these people around, showing them this and that, and they were making too much noise. My father was on the platform and he closed up his book and said, 'El que manda manda y yo me voy.' You know the phrase? It means 'Whoever is the boss is the boss, and I'm leaving.' By saying this he recognized the right of the owner to do what he wanted in his own factory, but he didn't have to stay around and put up with it. Then he walked out of the factory. When he left, the whole *gallera*—the shop—got up and followed him outside! It was one of those—what do you call it?— wildcat strikes. The owner had to beg my father to come back in. My father accepted his apology and returned, and only then did the workers come back.

"Such influence made the management nervous. There were quite a few strikes over the lectores. One time the management came in during the night and knocked down the lectores' stands. When the readers came in the morning, there was nothing there. The workers struck over that. In the early twenties the management wanted to bring in rolling machines, but they made so much noise the lector couldn't be heard. They struck and managed to get the new machines put in a different part of the building so the noise wouldn't interfere with the reading. During one of these strikes, my father moved the family back to Spain.

"That's how I came to live in Madrid from the time I was nine until I was eleven. It's funny, before I left Ybor City, the kids called me Henry. In Spain, they called me 'English' because I could speak English. In England, they called me 'Yankee.' When I returned to Ybor City, they called me *gallego,* which means 'Spanish hayseed.' I just used to say, 'Man, I'm an American!' After we moved back to Tampa, I continued to dress for a while in short pants like school-children do in Europe, and the kids called me—I don't want to say it—a bad word in Spanish for 'sissy.' But I adjusted pretty fast. My parents understood and let me wear long pants again.

"We got back in about 1926 and my father went back to being a lector, but by the early thirties mechanization could no longer be resisted and the days of the reader came to an end. It was hard for those who weren't as talented as my father. Some went back to Spain or Cuba and some had to suffer the comedown of becoming an ordi-nary cigar worker, who made much less money and didn't have the prestige. One man killed himself. He had no skill other than reading and was too depressed by the changing times.

"My father went on the radio with a program called 'The Span-ish Storyteller.' You know how they have pay television, now? We had pay radio. How could that be, you ask? Did people put money in the radio? No. It was something like what he'd done as a lector. Of course, anyone could listen to the program for free, but if you paid, I think it was fifty cents a week, you could vote on what my father would read on the show. We had about three hundred sub-scribers and every week my sister and I would go around and collect the money—like a paper route. My father could do this because he was so popular, but he was the exception. After a couple of years, Pet Milk began to sponsor the show, so we didn't have to have sub-scribers anymore. I still have examples of several big disks that the Pet Milk people had him make, which they sent around the country to be played in places where there were Spanish audiences.

"You'd have to do a whole book on my father to tell every-thing he did after he was a reader. He was a language expert for the United Nations and acted on the stage in New York. He had a long career with *Newsweek* magazine, interviewing world figures. He interviewed Castro in the mid-fifties and told me, 'He's a Commu-nist all the way. You'll find out.' My father's been dead for ten years now—more than ten years. All the lectores are dead.

"Ybor City is dead, too. Urban renewal turned it into a desert. They knocked down the houses and promised to help people rebuild, but they never did. So the people left. There's nobody here anymore. In its best days, you couldn't walk down Seventh Avenue, there were so many people, especially on Saturday. We'd go around and around and wave to each other. The boys would be walking down one side of the street and the girls on the other. They'd have chaperones or their mother or aunt or somebody. People were like ants, all over. The shops were open until two and three in the morning—the cafés and restaurants. You could leave your purse on the table and go over and talk to somebody and come back and the purse was there. Today, leave a purse anyplace, and it's gone!

"They say it's coming back, but I don't believe it will. At least I don't think I'll be alive to see it. I wish it would. I have memories. Very good memories."

—Interview by John Ames

Dempsey Barron

IN THE COURSE OF his turbulent political career, Dempsey Barron was called everything from a capricious rascal to a patriot, frequently by the same people. For thirty-two years, he was a fixture in the Florida legislature, a tenure that is the longest in the state's history and will probably remain so for all time. His political life spanned the period during which Florida went from a rural stronghold, controlled by a small group of good-old-boy politicians, to the fourth most populous state, one often cited as a model of fair apportionment.

First elected to public office in 1956, Dempsey Barron found upon his arrival in Tallahassee a legislature embattled over the civil rights issue. In his freshman year in the Florida house of representatives, he stepped forward to fight racist legislation designed to keep the state's policy of segregation in place. Considering that start, it is a tribute to his likability and powers of persuasion that he could manage to get reelected in Bay County, one of the most conservative districts in Florida.

In fact, most of Barron's races were close ones, since he never courted public approval on controversial issues. In the minds of some, he turned his back on his own kind when he authored the

first reapportionment plan in the nation to be approved by the U.S. Supreme Court, a plan that wrenched political control of the state from the hands of the notorious Pork Chop Gang, a handful of North Florida senators. He also led the movement for judicial reform, streamlining Florida's court system in spite of intense resistance from judges and other powerful special-interest groups. In 1982 he designed Florida's single-member districting plan, which resulted in the state's first black senator, its first Hispanic senator, and many more women in the legislature.

However, while he was frequently a supporter of legislation popular with liberals, his fiscal conservatism just as often alienated them. Though he was all for individual rights, he never felt that government should be given a blank check for social programs. His philosophy was to limit government's potential to abuse public funds by allotting it as little money as possible, a policy attacked by liberals as simplistic and reactionary. Typically, he was sometimes faulted for being far less prudent when it came to his pet projects.

In the early eighties, he further angered liberals by spearheading the defeat of the Equal Rights Amendment in Florida, attacking it as an ill-considered quick fix. The amendment's failure to make it through the Florida legislature killed its final chance of national adoption, earning Dempsey Barron praise from the right wing as the single most important figure in its defeat.

Though his attitudes often struck his colleagues as contradictory and he was known as a fearsome political enemy, most of his fellow legislators praise Barron as reliable in a very important regard: he didn't claim to be doing one thing when he was actually doing another. Though you might disagree with his reasoning or his conclusions, you could at least be sure he wasn't pursuing a secret agenda. Perhaps this characteristic explains why he was so often at the heart of coalitions joining unlikely political figures in a common cause. His consistent unwillingness to vote a party line and his political trustworthiness made him an invaluable facilitator and established his reputation as a power broker of the first order: during his long career, Dempsey Barron's name was prominently linked with a majority of the most controversial legislation taken up by the Florida senate.

In spite of his expertise and the apparent relish with which he went about his job, Barron refused to take a solemn attitude toward politics. Surveying the portraits of past presidents of the senate reveals that he is the only one who is portrayed as a cowboy on horseback—the rest are in business suits. That he would wish to be remembered to posterity as a cowboy is a fitting comment on the political style of a man who was widely quoted as once telling a governor, "Keep your damn hands off my senate!" His private life was likewise flamboyant. He claims to have "spilled more than most people have drunk," and political analysts have attributed his 1988 defeat in part to a divorce scandal.

When that defeat finally came, he expressed no regrets, indicating instead that he was in many ways relieved. Since that time, he claims that his health has improved dramatically and that he is enjoying life as never before. His private law practice has made him a man of means, and he divides his time between his ranch in North Florida and a much larger spread in Wyoming. Though officially retired, Dempsey Barron still has an impact on Florida's public affairs, occasionally using the respect and notoriety built up in his long career as leverage to influence issues that interest him. In this interview, he reveals something of the private man behind the political figure and also demonstrates the candor and wry humor that enlivened his public life.

"I WAS BORN IN Rose Hill, Alabama, which is probably less than fifty miles north of the Florida line. I don't recall ever being there. In 1922, my parents moved to what some people would call Panama City, but it was really Millville, Florida, which is the other side of the tracks from Panama City. And the reason it was named Millville, I assume, was because they had a big sawmill there named the German-American Lumber Company. I suspect that my daddy came down to Millville to try to get a job at that sawmill.

"I'm the third of seven children. My parents were working people, not very well educated. I doubt that either one of them got past the sixth grade in school. I stopped school myself in the fourth or fifth grade. We had at that time five children and no money. By then my daddy was a stevedore, which meant he only worked when the ships come in. We never had very much money because of the part-time work, nor did we have a lot of clothes or various things that you need. And one day I was going to school—frankly, I don't remember specifically about this, but I think I sort of remember it—and I was embarrassed because my clothes were not right somehow or other. Or shoes. Didn't have shoes or something. And I said I didn't want to go to school, and my mother said, 'Well, if that's the way you feel about it, just don't go back.' She had plenty of 'em to send to school, and my sisters were very good students. I think two of 'em were valedictorians of their class. They did well, and I just conned Mama into letting me stay home.

"It's hard to think of it in the context of today. There were a lot of people back then who didn't go to school. Now, I guess, there would be some laws or something, so that if you didn't go they'd get in touch with the parents and make 'em send their children. But there was nothing like that. It was a thousand years ago. I didn't miss it and didn't go back until after World War Two, when I found it was necessary to go to school, and I did that very rapidly.

"Before long, I was a developing young man. And I liked tough things, boxing and things like that. There was not much to do—going to western movies, sort of escaping to a better reality, with cowboys and ranches and interesting stories. That was on the weekends, but on weekdays, I worked if I could find work. I lived on the *other side* of the other side of the tracks. In fact, we lived in a black section near a dairy. Just about the first job I can remember ever having was at that dairy. After they milked the cows, the people at that dairy would turn the cows out to graze in the woods. It wasn't fenced or anything, and my job was to go out and stay with 'em, and drive 'em back up by foot at the end of the day. For fifty cents a day. That job and western movies were probably the beginning of my interest in ranching.

"By the time I was fifteen, I was working at a dock where barges came in with loads of food—sacks of sugar and corn, cooking oil, syrup—and all other kinds of things people use. These barges would come into a place not far from where I lived. You got paid by the hour, and you would work as long as it took to do it. There was no going to work at a certain time and coming back. When the tugboats brought the barges in, you'd go down and work, and I remember working thirty-six hours one time, nonstop. This was very hard labor. You'd go down a gangplank and walk from down on the barge up to the warehouses, and carry stuff on your shoulder: hundred-pound sacks of flour, beans, and seed, various things that they had. And I remember they had two big black men who would lift the load up— we were like a line of slaves—and you'd walk up there and they'd put it on you, then the next guy. Then you'd walk up that gangplank. People would just pass out from working. And everybody wanted, *had* to work: there was just no jobs. It was in the middle of the Depression. And I'd come up, and one of those black fellows, I remember him saying, 'Here's one that can take it!' It would make me feel great. And I remember after working thirty-six hours—it was hot as hell, and the dock was on a bayou—I jumped in the bayou and swam across and back, just to prove I was still alive.

"Then Roosevelt started the Civilian Conservation Corps. They called it the CCC. Young men could go away somewhere and work. I went, I think, when I was about sixteen. I think you had to be seventeen to go . . . if it was eighteen, I was seventeen. Anyway, I was one year under the minimum, and I went to Medford, Oregon, the furthest place in the world, to work in the forest out there. You wore uniforms, like khakis, and it was cold, but I felt like I was seeing the world: the prettiest part of the country. I probably had never been more than fifty miles from Millville, prior to that time. You got to work and have money and go into town on Saturday night. It was very similar to military service, which is where I wound up shortly after I left the CCC.

"I came back to Millville, and the Japanese bombed Pearl Harbor, and I did like millions of other Americans: I signed up. There was a lot of jingoism and patriotism. They talked about how we'd run over there and whip those Japs in about three weeks and be back home. So I joined the navy, and wound up on the *USS Chicago* as a gunner on a twenty-millimeter. It's one of those guns where you strap yourself into it and shoot at enemy aircraft. The *Chicago* was a big ship, eight hundred and fifty feet long, and carried thirteen hundred and fifty men. We were in a convoy with a bunch of liberty ships carrying guns and men out there in the Pacific. We were always on alert, but we were expecting the enemy about eight o'clock one night, or at least there was talk among us that the Japs might be comin' tonight at eight. Now, the person that knows the least about a war is the guy that's in it. He is absolutely the least important guy in the world, especially if he's an enlisted man. You don't sit down and have strategy and all that. You just go shoot those guns. You don't know if you're winning or losing. You know if you're living or dying, and that's all you know. So, I hadn't paid too much attention to the rumors and I was down below decks at eight o'clock, writing in my diary, when they sounded 'general quarters.' That's a very awesome, scary sound. They make it be scary, I think. It's a thing going, 'Ooogah! Ooogah! Ooogah!' And I finished writing in my diary before going up topside and, hell, five minutes later a torpedo came right in that place where I'd been. But we got up there and got shot by the Japanese, and they were coming in with torpedo planes. A torpedo was the most devastating weapon in World War Two. They got something worse now, but the torpedo was the wolf then. A big long thing that lived by itself, alone. It didn't have to have any support. When they hit the water, they had a little propeller, and they just went where you sent 'em. In the course of the battle, one of the planes we shot down hit a great big old radar we had sticking up from the top of the ship, fell over the side, and burst into flames. With all the fuel on the water, it lit up the world and the Japs just blew us away. We got four torpedoes that night. It wasn't one of those glorious things that you see in the movies. People are scared. But we didn't sink that night, and the next morning we got towed.

"About four o'clock in the afternoon, the Japs came back, and that boat that was towing us just cut the line and left, which is what they were supposed to do, 'cause they're supposed to maneuver and avoid being hit. I saw the torpedoes coming. I saw four torpedoes—you can see 'em because they make a wake. They just blew us to hell. When a torpedo hits a ship, it just goes way up in the air, like a tarpon, and when it comes down it shakes. I wasn't especially happy, but frankly, I wasn't as scared as those other guys (most of 'em), because they were afraid of the ocean. Hell, I could swim in the ocean, I knew that. But those other kids, they were afraid they were gonna drown.

"That situation taught me something about human nature, because

I just kinda took over. There were no officers or anything around. You know, in the movies the captain says, 'Abandon ship,' but we had no communications. Our phones were gone. Everything was blown out. The ship obviously was gonna sink, and these people were just standing around. We had a bunch of cots on the ship for the men we were gonna land on Guadalcanal, and they had a lot of wood in 'em, so I'd just go up to people, hand 'em one, and say, 'Here, take this cot and jump overboard.' In a situation like that, human nature is such that people will do exactly what you tell 'em to do.

"Once I was out in the water myself, I thought, 'I bet those guys come back and strafe us,' which they usually did, so I took off my Mae West life vest and threw it away. I wanted to be able to dive. They put out lifeboats to pick up people and take them to other ships, and they tried to pick me up but I wouldn't get picked up. I wanted them to pick up those guys that were scared of the water. I was more afraid of getting blown up, and I knew that couldn't happen as long as I was in the water. I knew that I could swim forever. I used to go swimming when I was ten years old, and I probably swam six hours without ever going back to the land. I know this sounds crazy, but I was patriotic and tough and I was singing and stuff, in the water.

"Eventually, ships came and picked us up, and I got picked by a ship with a crew of a hundred and twenty-five and there were *two hundred and something* of us. Then we were on that thing for four days, and that was the worst part of the war, because there were so many of us that we couldn't go below, and they had a bunch of hurt people below, anyway. And I was thin-skinned and covered in oil from the wrecked ship and the damn sun just about burned me to pieces. You couldn't get in the shade, you know.

"They took us to New Caledonia, a French-possessed island, where I recovered. I stayed there a year and ended up teaching gunnery at a gunnery school. I thought my staying there was a great injustice. I thought I'd made it through a hot war and one person shouldn't have to do it over and over again, and that I should be sent back to America so I could go to New York City and start chasing women. Eventually they did ship me back and sent me to gunnery school in Washington D.C., where I suffered the second greatest injustice that ever happened in my life: they sent me to night school after all the girls got off from work!

"There's a lot that could be said about the war. I guess it was the most significant thing that happened in my life, but when I got out of the service I had no education, no skills that you could use in the civilian world. They were building a paper mill in Pensacola, and I went to work there as a steel worker. I used to go home on weekends and one night I was coming home and they stopped the bus in Fort Walton. I got off the bus, stepped in a pothole, and twisted my ankle. Damn near ruined it. I went on home, and the bus people knew that I hurt my ankle, so I got a call a day or two later from a lawyer named Warren Fitzpatrick. And he wanted me to come see him. He was the attorney for the insurance company of this bus line. And he didn't want to get sued, you know, even though you didn't do that back then like people do now. So he asked me to come by his office and I did. He told me that they were gonna pay the doctor bills, and how much time was I gonna lose from work? And how much more money did he owe me? I thought, 'Man, he's paying me not to work!' Anyway, he paid me and got a release—that's what he wanted.

"After about a year, I decided that I really wasn't going anywhere and that I really needed some education. By that time they had come out with the GED tests to repay service men who hadn't finished school. So I took those multiple-guess tests, but I hadn't been to school since the fourth grade and I knew I'd never be able to pass the math, so I said I'd come back later for that one. Well, in the Navy I had gone to electric-hydraulic school and, knowing that I didn't know anything, studied hard and finished first in my class. And they gave me a diploma that said that. So I took that to the principal of Bay High School where they administered the GED and quoted Pascal's Law and said some other things that made it sound like I knew something, and he let me substitute it for the math. That gave me a high school degree, and I took the entrance exam at FSU and passed that, but I had to cram four years of undergraduate work and three years of law school into four years, because that was all the GI Bill would pay for. With a little creative scheduling, I was able to do that, though the administration at FSU was not too happy when they discovered what I was up to. But I made it.

"I came back to Panama City, and the only fellow I knew in the world was that fellow Fitzpatrick, who paid me that money for nothing, for stepping off the bus. So, I went to see him, and he badly needed a new lawyer, so he hired me. But I didn't know anything. I was embarrassed to try to dictate to secretaries, because I had no formal . . . anything. And I'd stay down at the office at night and write all of my reports out. So he thought I was the hardest-working fellow alive, and I was just trying to learn. He was having a really bad divorce and going through a bunch of other stuff, so in about three weeks, he said, 'Well, you're doing pretty good. Would you like to be a partner?' And I said, 'Yeah, it'd be all right with me.' So he made me a partner. Just the two of us.

"Along about that time, a good friend I grew up with came by and said, 'Look, they're signing up people to run for the house of representatives. There's two seats in Bay County. Why don't we run for 'em?' I said, 'What is it? How do you spell it?' Finally I said, 'I don't care. You really wanna do it?' and he said, 'Yeah,' so we went down and registered to run. I didn't even know where Tallahassee was. I really did, but . . .

"I drew the toughest opponent in the world. He was the guy on radio that gave everybody the weather and the news, twice, three times a day. Knew all the business people in town. But TV was just beginning up there and you could buy thirty minutes for about twice as much as you could buy five minutes. (It costs a billion dollars now.) So, I'd buy a thirty-minute program, sit down and talk about things, get up and walk around, tell stories, recite poetry. Got a few people and we all went to workin' like hell. First primary, there were three of us in the race (one of 'em was a former house member), and that newscaster came within two, three hundred votes of beating us *both*.

"Well, I'd been out practicing law, and I'd walk down the street and I'd had some little old cards made, and I'd see people and I'd say, 'I'm running for the house of representatives,' and they'd say, 'Good luck, son!' I thought that meant they were gonna vote for me! I didn't know that didn't mean nothing. After the primary, I said to myself, 'God, these people are liars!' I thought I was gonna get every vote in town! They even had a victory party for my opponent that night. He pronounced that he had won the election, but three weeks later in the second primary, I won.

"I attribute it to television, 'cause I could buy that television time so cheap and get my message out. That and the two-primary system. This is the way I did it. I'd say,

Folks, I'm Dempsey Barron and I'm runnin' for the house of rep-
resentatives. I'm out there workin' and my friends are workin'.
I'd like to go over there and speak for you. I hope there's some-
thing I can do. You know I've got a house and a dog and a boat
and they're all paid for, and I don't owe anybody any money.
Never have stole anything or taken advantage of anyone that
was lesser than I was. I believe in treatin' people right and bein'
treated right, and for laws to be enacted that are consistent with
that kind of philosophy: bein' honest and speakin' out on sub-
jects that are important to you. I think that if you get born in
this country, grow up and get the GI Bill like I did, and you get
the opportunity to get an education, and if the system and the
people and the government and the philosophy of the country
where you live contributes to helping you to do that, then you
should try to do something to contribute to making better laws
and fairer laws, and give people equality under the law. We need
to do more than just pass through here. If you're passing along a
difficult path, and you come to a river and you can't get across,
and you find a bridge, then you know that somebody that came
by there before you must have built that bridge. It's like that bridge
builder. Somebody wrote a poem about him one time. Let me see
if I can remember it.

An old man traveling a long highway,
Came at the end of the closing day
To a chasm vast and deep and wide
He stopped when safe on the other side
To build a bridge and span the tide.
'Old man', said a pilgrim standing near,
'You're wasting your time building here
Your journey will end with the closing day,
And you never again will pass this way.'

The builder lifted his old gray head.
'My friend, on the path I have come,' he said,
'There follows after me today,
A youth who too must pass this way.
While this chasm has been as naught to me,
To that fair-haired youth it may a pitfall be.

He too must pass in the twilight dim.
Good friend, I'm building this bridge for him.'

I think that's a pretty good philosophy.

"That was the kind of stuff I did on television. Anyway, I guess it worked.

"I had tried court cases and stuff, so I was never in awe of the legislature, even though it was of a much higher quality then. In fact, I'm pretty much ashamed of our state government now. We had the best freshman class my first term by far—twice as good—as any that I ever saw, and I was there thirty-two years. There were about forty of us. Leroy Collins was governor of Florida. The world was afire with the racial issue. Martin Luther King was marching. The legislature was chaotic and was responding to the U.S. Supreme Court's ruling on integration in the most explosive and irresponsible way. They passed laws in the Florida house of representatives, over the strong objections of myself and most of those freshmen representatives, that said if one black child was admitted to a white school, they would go around and take a vote in the area affected, and if the people voted to, they could close the schools. They called it the Last Resort Bill. Well, that was just an invitation to a riot. They passed laws to take welfare away from black mothers, especially unwed mothers, and I made a stirring speech about starving black children. They passed a law in the house that said that if you owned a motel and you let a black person stay in it as a guest, you had to put a sign up, as big as the biggest sign you had. (It was an old fellow from DeFuniak that introduced the bill.) And the sign—let's say you had a Holiday Inn; that sign, you know, is as big as this ceiling—you had to have an equal-sized sign flashing off and on saying, 'Integrated! Integrated! Integrated!' That was the kind of stuff they were doing. Collins vetoed it, but they overrode it quickly in the senate. We took it up in the house and sustained his veto by one vote.

"I think I'm the only person in this part of the country that voted with the governor. And I had the damndest race you ever saw the next time. Back then, the black people sold their votes to the sheriff (many of them still do), so he controls them, and all the blacks voted against me and all the rednecks voted against me. How in the hell I survived, I don't know. Anyway, that was my introduction to the legislature.

"I'm a liberal with regard to human rights, and I always have been. I authored the first reapportionment bill that ever passed muster in the Supreme Court of the United States. It gave equal rights to all people based on one-person-one-vote. And that's quite an accomplishment. I passed laws that required equal pay for equal work for women, especially in government and universities and that kind of thing. The thing that confuses people is that I'm a conservative on taxing people. I think government is bad, almost in all regards. It's the most inefficient way in the world to do things. It has no relationship to the wise expenditure of extracted tax dollars. It has no managerial programs or plan. The government produces no measurable product; therefore, you can't ever tell if money's spent wisely. So the only way you can control the overexpansion of government, and permit people to keep the money that they earn, is to withhold funds from it, and don't keep throwing more tax money at everything that comes along. There's a legitimate need for government. You gotta have it to educate people, and you gotta have it for law enforcement, and you gotta have it to transport poor people around. But there's a billion public programs that should be weeded out of government. So, I'm conservative with regard to taking people's money, unless you can prove that it's needed and that you're using it wisely.

"One thing that confuses the liberals is that I voted against the Equal Rights Amendment. In fact *I* beat it in Florida, alone: the last state. It's certainly not my proudest accomplishment, but it's damn high on my personal agenda. I was opposed to the Equal Rights Amendment because it was too vague and too quick-sell, and it had too many potential flaws in it. At the time we were debating the Equal Rights Amendment, people were talking about doing away with the Girl Scouts and the Boy Scouts! Doing away with girls' schools and boys' schools. Well, personally, if I was going to school I'd prefer it to be where you had a coed-type deal, but other folks, if they wanna go to something different, they should have the right to do that. And I don't care what they say, I don't think it's an even match-up— although women do it in some places—but I don't wanna put a hundred-and-twenty-pound woman in the front lines on the way to

Moscow in that damn winter that the Germans tried out over there. Now, I want all the women to do whatever the hell they want to, and the men too, including joining the military service, but as somewhat of a scholar of the law, that Equal Rights Amendment was a quick fix that was easy to say 'yes' to. But if you didn't agree with it, they said you must be anti-rights. And it was just the other way with me. I can't ever convince people of that, nor do I give a damn. I knew what I thought. That's the position I took: Did it then, would do it again. At the same time, I was *sponsoring* laws for equal pay for women and equal opportunity for women. Specific things that we knew what it said and what it meant. I didn't think that the Equal Rights Amendment was nearly as important as people tried to make it.

"I have a friend who agonizes over every vote. I didn't do that, and it shows politically at times. There was a job to do over there, and I just did the job the best way I knew how. Whatever the hell anybody writes about it or concludes about it, well, I have no control over that. There are certain places you can go where all you gotta do in order to get recognized is go around filling the vacuums, like I filled the vacuum in leadership on the *Chicago* back during the war, and there were a lot of vacuums to be filled over in the legislature. I filled 'em."

—Interview by John Ames

FORT LAUDERDALE

Tomotsu Kobayashi

A LITTLE-KNOWN CHAPTER IN Florida history is evidenced by the intersection of Yamato Road and Route 95 near Boca Raton. Yamato, the ancient name for Japan, is a reminder of a small party of Japanese expatriates who came to Florida in 1904 to homestead pineapple plantations and vegetable truck farms. The men who came over were seeking economic freedom from Japan's primogeniture system. Once established in Delray Beach, they sent for Japanese women to marry, and the colony grew.

The Yamato colony thrived until the 1940s, when World War II erupted and Pearl Harbor was bombed. The colony's land was confiscated by the federal government under laws of eminent domain to make way for a military base, and a new road, Military Trail, soon crossed Yamato Road.

Hundreds of thousands of American Japanese were interned in military camps during the war upon President Franklin Roosevelt's Executive Order 9066. In Florida, homes of the relatively few Japanese living in the state were searched for contraband, and each family was assigned a navy escort who lived with them in their homes.

Tomotsu Kobayashi, who was born in Florida in 1927 to Hideo and

Photo by Henry Rowland

Umeko—founding members of the Yamato colony—remembers the navy escort his family was assigned, but makes light of the experience. Like most second-generation immigrants, he has blended into the American culture and feels truly at home in Fort Lauderdale, where he works as a landscaper. He sometimes visits the Morikami Museum in Delray, which today houses artifacts from the colony in a traditional Japanese-style home, complete with bonsai trees, carp pond, and meditation garden.

"I WAS BORN IN BOCA RATON. My father was Hideo Kobayashi. He was born in Kinosaki, Japan, in 1883. He died in 1967. My mother was Umeko Kono. She was born in 1897 and died in 1984.

"My father came here with the Yamato homesteaders in 1907. Jo Saki convinced Henry Flagler in 1903 to back Japanese settlers. He said they would drain and cultivate the land around Flagler's railroad.

"About forty bachelors came to South Florida, after landing in Seattle and California. Creditors lended money for the trip. The creditors were paid back as cash crops were sold. Eventually the settlers owned their own land. It was never a commune here. Everyone worked for themselves.

"Of course, in the early days they weren't allowed to own property. Aliens in the 1920s and 1930s were forbidden. In 1927 my Dad had his own land by forming the H. Kobayashi Company with an American named Ben Sunday. Ben was stockholder and vice-president. Dad was president, and my mother was treasurer. They grew peppers, beans, and squash and sold the produce to local markets and northern cities.

"The Japanese came over because, as in Europe, there was a primogeniture system in Japan. The eldest brother took over the household when the father died. All the other brothers had to work for him. Those who rebelled left to come to America and start lives for themselves.

"Originally the Yamato settlement grew pineapples. The land was cleared of slash pines and cabbage palms using grub hoes. The men worked from sunup to sundown. It was hard.

"Competition from Cuban growers and blight forced out most of the pineapple plantations. To survive, the men tried truck farming in the Boca and Pompano areas around Dixie Highway. It was just a dirt road before Route One was constructed in the 1930s.

"George Sukeji Morikami was a pioneer from that era. He was born in 1896 in Miyazu, Japan, and was one of the early settlers of the Yamato colony with my father. He became a wholesale vegetable farmer.

"Morikami finally became a citizen in 1971 when he learned he could afford it. He died a millionaire and donated his land to Palm Beach County. The county built the Morikami Museum of Japanese Culture on the donated land. They brought over Japanese artisans and Miyazu was made a sister city of Delray Beach as a goodwill gesture.

"We also knew the Frank Kamiya family (he was a chef) and the Jinzo Yamauchi family (he was a landscape gardener in Miami Beach). Eventually others became nursery farmers in Miami Beach or moved on to Pahokee, Okeechobee, Jacksonville and other parts of the country. One became a Ford designer in Detroit. Others became gardeners, salesmen, or opened Japanese restaurants. We all became part of the American heritage.

"In 1920 my father returned to Japan to marry. It was arranged for him by the families. It was hard for my mother to come back with him. Florida was still wilderness. She had to deal with mosquitoes, heat, and a new culture.

"My parents never became citizens. They couldn't vote. Some lawyer told them it would cost over six thousand dollars. This, of course, wasn't true. My brother and sister and I are *issie*—first generation. They were born Americans in the Yamato colony. We had three acres. When my dad first came over, he lived in a tent. He built a shack like those living in Colored Town. Gradually he built a modest house, American style, with a large porch in front. Everyone in the colony helped each other build houses.

"Japanese houses with paper walls were no good in Florida because humidity will mildew them. Today all that remains of our old property is a mango tree and a dam in an irrigation canal near where Florida Atlantic University is today. I used to play in the mango tree.

"My dad used to have a Model-A truck. My mother was five-foot-two-inches tall, and when she learned to drive, she had to sit on the edge of the seat to reach the pedals and clutch-release lever.

"My parents picked up English along the way. They never went to American school for education. All of us colonists were assimilated into the culture like the Germans who lived in Delray.

"I remember we used to buy green tea from the Food Fair grocery store. My mother had simple tea ceremonies. When we'd invite out American friends they thought it was real Japanese tea!

"My dad was a conscientious fisherman who caught minnows just before sunrise by 'Jap Rock.' Because of shifting sands it's almost buried in the ocean today. He fished with a grape box, strapping it around his neck. It hung on his chest. Instead of a rod and reel he wound string into the box.

"We used minnows as bait to catch snappers, blue runners, and jacks. Fish were plentiful then. You could fill hundred-pound feed sacks in three hours. I remember putting silver minnows out to dry in the sun on the corrugated tin roof of the washing shed. When the fish dried out, we'd crumple them over our salads for flavoring. Japanese and Eskimos do this.

"On Sundays after church we came home and cranked up the ice cream machine. My mother used vanilla extract and everything. We used kerosene lanterns and iceboxes from the 1930s through 1941. Only the Kamiya family had electricity.

"I recall Colored Town. We bartered fish for big chunks of bologna at Montgomery's General Store near there in Yamato. Colored sharecroppers helped us in the fields during harvest. Colored repairmen worked on the Florida East Coast Railway to fix the tracks. The foreman was white.

"The locomotives were steam engines that used water from big water tanks south of Yamato Road. We children used to play in the ditches by the side of the tracks when they filled with rainwater.

"In 1942, after the war broke out, the government moved us off our property. They only gave us half-value of what the land was worth. We didn't know how to fight it. They made the property into a big military base for B-24 bombers. It stretched from the Florida East Coast Railroad track to where Military Trail is today.

"Japanese on the west coast of America were put in detention camps during the war. Here Coast Guard boys lived with us on twelve-hour shifts. They accompanied us shopping and we had to house and feed them. They helped the government if there was trouble and they helped protect us too. So it worked two ways.

"It was funny. One of the boys with us had a German father living in New York. We were both American citizens but I was being watched by him. In the meantime German U-boats were sinking American ships.

"We had no trouble. I do recall the FBI searching our house. They found an old Morse code kit we used to play with in the attic. It was confiscated 'cause they thought we might send signals to the German U-boats. The signals could only travel a mile!

"We knew there was a war on and accepted our situation in it. My oldest brother even applied to serve as a turret gunner on a B-17 bomber. He was short but wasn't accepted because of a fractured elbow. But a whole regiment of Japanese-Americans did serve in the war. I was sent to Okinawa in the South Pacific. I guarded Japanese prisoners of war. I spent over twenty years in the U.S. Army reserves.

"In 1937 my Dad sold the farms he had left and became a landscape gardener. We moved to Fort Lauderdale in 1941 and I learned landscape gardening, which is my occupation today."

—Interview by William Pohl

Photo by Henry Rowland

Dorothy Conner Shipes

IN A GOOD YEAR, Dorothy Conner Shipes can step off her front porch, walk a few feet, and pick oranges from trees that have been bearing fruit for nearly a century. Her family has been a part of Central Florida's citrus industry since the Big Freeze of 1895 forced her grandfather to move his nursery business south from Oklawaha. Though the family company retains the name Ocklawaha Nurseries (with the original, unmodernized spelling), its property has been devoted exclusively to groves for more than forty years. Since the death of her father, Dorothy Conner Shipes's responsibility in running the family business has steadily increased, and she is now the final authority. As her prominence in the family business has grown, so also has her prominence in the industry at large, and she has been awarded numerous posts, including a seat on the board of directors of Florida Citrus Mutual and both the directorship and the presidency of the Lake County Farm Bureau. She was only the second woman in history to be appointed to membership on the Florida Citrus Commission, and in 1987 she was named Florida's Woman of the Year in Agriculture. Her soft-spoken and unassuming manner disguises her considerable strength, which has been evident as, like her

Photo by Walter Michot

grandfather before her, she has faced natural disaster and refused to knuckle under.

As a result of catastrophic freezes in December 1983 and January 1985, much of the once-luxuriant grove area along the Orange Blossom Trail north of Orlando now lies blasted, either covered with dead trees or bulldozed flat in anticipation of future development: the cost of replanting and the seductively high land prices in the Disney World area have combined to squelch the rejuvenation of the citrus industry in Orange County. But Dorothy Conner Shipes insisted on replanting and by 1989, kept afloat by disaster loans and the produce from old trees which had been saved by their proximity to the warmth of Lake Jem, she had put behind her most of the six-year wait that growers must endure before young trees bear fruit. Her interview—done at that time—reflects the optimism of the moment. Then, over Christmas of 1989, she and the rest of Central Florida's remaining growers received an unwelcome gift: another devastating cold snap, which froze Ocklawaha Nurseries' new trees so severely that they will take six more years to become productive. Even the reliable old trees are in doubt. Their root systems were unquestionably damaged by the two earlier freezes and this latest one may have diminished them beyond hope of any crop in the near future. Time will tell. Meanwhile, unless a miracle occurs, some portion of the 550 acres comprising the family's grove land will have to be sold in order to finance another six years of waiting.

Shipes's comments on the Christmas freeze reflect her frustration. "It's one thing to lose your job," she said, "but this is like losing five years of your life." However, in spite of this setback, she remains determined to save something of the citrus tradition which has for a hundred years characterized both her family and her Central Florida home.

"MY GRANDFATHER CAME TO FLORIDA in the late 1800s from the Kentucky-Tennessee area. From what I can find out, he was a teacher up there and decided to come to Florida, and I guess was enchanted with the state as it was then. He got into buying and selling property, plants and groves and things like that. He started his nursery business in the little town of Oklawaha, but he moved down here to the Tangerine–Lake Jem area after the freeze in 1895. That was kind of interesting, because back then they didn't have the facilities—like irrigation—that we have now to fight the cold, and when he heard that this frigid mass of air was moving in, he went into his nurseries with his mules and plowed furrows to cut the roots on one side of his little trees. Then he pushed them down and covered them over with dirt. And that was the way he saved his nursery and was able to recoup after the Big Freeze.

"When he moved here, he married my grandmother, who was from New Smyrna Beach. At that time, this area was super-remote, and she used to tell about how it would take them two days to get to New Smyrna. They would go from here to the Saint Johns and camp overnight and go on the next day to the coast. A lot of the land that we own was bought for practically nothing because it was so remote. Then more was added during the Bust when you could buy it just for the taxes. The house that my grandfather and grandmother built in Tangerine is still standing. It's a little two-story, typical country-style Florida house, with the porches around it. When they moved over here to this side of Lake Jem, they built a small wooden Florida Cracker house, but there weren't any major roads out this way, so their children used to go to school in Mount Dora by 'motor launch,' as they called it. In fact, the motor launch was the way the family did its main shopping. A couple of times a year they'd go to Jacksonville. And my grandmother would tell about how if the water was low—because then there weren't locks to regulate the fall of water—that they'd hit sandbars and have to get out of the launch and push it off. So it must have been quite adventuresome.

"My grandfather died in the flu epidemic during the First World War. My grandmother was a spunky woman and decided that she was not going to lose everything, so she rolled up her sleeves and got busy. She ran the business, which at that time was primarily nurseries. I guess it was a pretty rough life for a woman back then. Women generally didn't participate a lot, but my grandmother handled all aspects of the business, and she slowly built the groves. Then as the company grew and my father grew up, she and he together opened a packinghouse to pack the fruit that the groves produced. My grandmother died when she was eighty-three, and during her lifetime, she went from going by horse and buggy to New Smyrna Beach to seeing a man launched to the moon from Cape Canaveral. Those trees you saw on the left out there? They were planted when she first came here and are still producing after a hundred years.

"Even as a child, I felt a certain amount of pride at harvest time, a certain amount of excitement when I began to see the pickers in the groves. After all these years it's still exciting for me when it gets to be that time of year. I think my father passed that along to his children. He was always enthusiastic. All the children were encouraged to take an interest in the business if we showed any desire. I can remember walking through the grove with my father. He always would say, 'Look, baby, there's a bug that's called a so-and-so, and it's a problem,' or 'We need to put fertilizer over there.' You know, he just shared his knowledge in a kind of casual and conversational way.

"I was always interested in what was going on and enjoyed watching the workers. I can remember watching the men bud trees, and one of the things that comes back to memory is that they would do what they would call 'hunker down.' Nowadays, they take a little stool to sit on, but at that time they'd squat for hours on end. Then you'd see them come out of the grove and maybe they'd be talking among themselves, and here they'd be all squatting again! That has always pegged in my memory, because if you've ever squatted, you know how tired your legs get and how quickly you're ready to get up. Seeing things like that gave me a good understanding of how hard grove work is. I'm still inclined to pay laborers more than somebody who sits in an office.

"The family children had the opportunity to participate in all aspects of the business. We were permitted to hang around the packinghouse, and if we were interested we could pack fruit. It was fun. When the fruit comes through it's sized into bins, and then according to what size it is, you place it in a box in a pattern. Later, about twenty years ago, I operated the packinghouse myself, after I came back and started working in the company.

"But for quite some time, I was away from the groves. That period of my life started when I was sent away to finish my last two years of schooling in Virginia. Yes, it was a 'finishing school.' We were still in that period when we 'finished' women, and I was married shortly after graduation to a navy pilot. For many years we lived all over the United States, anywhere there was a navy base. Eventually, he retired and we came back to Florida, but it was after my father died in the late sixties that I actually became involved in running the business. Then, after my grandmother died a few years later, I took on more responsibility.

"I had been helping out in the office and with the bookkeeping and then all of a sudden I found myself responsible for the whole thing, growing, harvesting, all of it. I knew that I had to get an education and quickly. I soon discovered that it wasn't enough to just know how to grow fruit. You have to know what's going on in the citrus community. You need to know where the best places are to buy fertilizer and supplies, and, in the marketing end, where to go to sell your fruit and get a good price. One of the best ways to make these contacts is to attend the meetings of citrus organizations. For many years I was the only woman there. And at first the men would kind of—Is she waiting table or what? I'm kidding, of course. They weren't that bad, but they were kind of surprised that I was there. I persisted in going, because there's a lot of things to be learned at those meetings through seminars that the university puts on and things like that. It was a couple of years before the men began to speak to me as a peer. I think it was the fact that I was constantly visible and that I began to understand more. Now, to tell the truth, I'm more comfortable talking business with those men than I am with the women that are beginning to show up more and more frequently. It's just a matter of learning to speak the language, and that takes some time.

"The biggest catastrophe to hit the industry this century was the recent freezes in 1983 and '85. At Ocklawaha Nurseries we lost, I'd say, seventy-five percent of our groves. We've had freezes before, but nothing as devastating as this freeze, which actually killed the trees, split them wide open.

"That night I couldn't sleep, because I realized what was happening. I sat right there on that couch. This freeze was accompanied by a wind that howled, and I just sat there all night long and listened to that wind. I can remember as a child, we did have occasional problems with cold weather and they would burn woodpiles and tires and make the smoke that would keep the frost from settling. For those of us at home, it was kind of a fun thing, because we'd all get in the kitchen and cook soup, and we'd take it out to the men in the fields. But this freeze was nothing like that. There's no closeness or camaraderie in a freeze where you're just getting flat-out frozen.

"I thought about what might be done. Maybe say to heck with the environment and go out and burn old rubber tires or something, but that wind was so high that it wouldn't have done any good: the smoke would have been blown away. My son that works with me was like a caged tiger. He was in and out, riding around, calling me on the radio with the latest from the area weather stations. There was nothing you could do. It was just an impossible situation.

"The bad thing was the duration of the cold. That's what killed the trees. It was down well below freezing for twenty-four hours or more. Temperatures in the teens. Temperatures that we had never seen before. In the morning, there was not only frost, there was ice. The wind was so ferocious that it blew a spray from the lake, and everything along the lake front had an ice coating on it. I had never, ever seen anything like it, except when we lived in the North. As soon as it got to be daylight, we cut fruit to see which had ice in it, and of course it all did. In fact, there was some fruit that we could bounce off the sidewalk, it was so hard. Just frozen solid.

"A year later, when the second freeze came, it was the same type of thing, the way that cold front moved in with that howling wind. And I thought, 'Oh, God. This can't happen again.' But it did.

"We had lost a majority of our trees in that first freeze, but some had started to come back out. In fact we really felt that a lot of them would come back. We thought, 'Well, we've lost some, but we're still in good shape. In a couple of years we'll be back in production, because the trees will leaf out and we'll get fruit.' But when the second one came, the growth was so tender that the trees just turned toes up, and that was it.

"It's an unbelievable feeling. One day you've got something and the next day you just don't have anything!

"The hardest decisions I've made in this business came in having to let people go after the freeze. That really wrenched my heart-strings, because, you know, even among the pickers that come and go, there are always some that come every year, and to have to say, 'We're sorry. We don't have any work,' that's hard. My son told some of his friends, 'You know things are bad when your *mother* fires you.' He had been doing mechanical work for the company, and we just couldn't afford to keep him on. Luckily, he went back to school to study computers, and he's happy doing that now, so in his case it turned out for the best.

"The freeze left a lot of people totally discouraged. And they really were very opposed to getting back into growing. But there was a group of us that got together at the Farm Bureau (I'm on the board of directors over in Lake County) and got to discussing the plight of the citrus growers and how everybody was having negative thoughts about replanting. So, we just thought that we should start pumping people up a little bit, start showing some of the positive side of what would happen if you replanted. So we got with the University of Florida and some other people who project patterns of weather, and we put on a big seminar-type thing and invited growers down. We got a packed house and wound up doing three or four sessions like that on various aspects of the situation. We did some talking about disaster loans and how to replant close-set groves for higher yields. People began to think that, well, maybe it wasn't a total wipeout after all. Maybe there were things that could be done. After that, we began to see people get back into the swing of things, and there has been quite a bit of replanting.

"Our area up here, historically, has been composed of a lot of small groves. Now, you don't find that down south of Orlando. They're big growers and they'll plant a grove that's a thousand acres. Up here we had a lot of small twenty-five-acre, hundred-acre-type groves that belonged to the everyday individual. And for them to have to go back and replant—it's expensive. When you've got a crop like we've got, it's not like being a vegetable farmer, where you can go back and replant and be harvesting in three or four months. You have to wait five or six years before new trees begin producing, and in the meantime, the fertilizers and insecticides are so expensive that you're putting out bundles of money to get going. A lot of the growers are retirees, too, and I can imagine how they felt. It must have really pulled at the heartstrings. Do I make this investment again, or do I just leave the land lay and when development reaches it, sell? That money from developers down the line is a big factor. We're twenty-three miles out from Orlando here, and I really don't think we'll see groves re-planted much closer than that.

"Our company is operating right now on a disaster loan. Getting it was quite involved, and I can tell you that I filled out three or four boxes of papers. Ours is through the Small Business Administration. They do put a mortgage on your property, but the bonds are long-term, like twenty-five years, and they're at a four percent interest rate, which helps a farmer. For the first three years, we didn't have to pay anything back. We've managed it so far, mainly because we hadn't reached that period where payback began. And we're coping with it now, but you know it's hard to continue to operate with a lot of grove that's not producing. The grove that is producing is not making enough to care for everything, and we've got another year or two before we get to a break-even point.

"To replant was a decision that took some thought, but in look-ing at the history of the citrus industry and looking at the history of freezes in Florida—well, so it freezes in another hundred years! My grandfather was hurt by the Big Freeze, but it didn't stop him from replanting. There's a certain excitement and a certain reward to being a citrus grower. You watch the trees grow and you watch them bloom, and then when you get to the period in the winter when you pick the fruit, it's exciting to see what you've done. The reward is not all money. There's a sense of accomplishment. And it's just some-thing that I couldn't resist. If you've ever been a citrus grower, you're always a citrus grower. It's just in your blood."

—Interview by John Ames

Janetta Giles Norman

JANETTA GILES NORMAN is one of many black Floridians who grew to adulthood under a policy of segregation. Though she speaks of the bitterness she felt toward the system, there is surprisingly little bitterness in her voice now. When the system changed, she was willing to give the new order a chance and to make a fresh start; however, she carries with her the lessons of those times, when opportunities and role models for blacks were scarce.

She maintains that her success as an academic and an educator is largely due to the influence of involved people who took a personal interest in her when society at large did not. She judges herself extremely lucky to have found at an early age people who inspired her to value education and to believe in herself. That inspiration eventually led her to a master's degree in education from the University of Florida and a doctorate in education from Nova University.

She remembered the importance of inspiration when she took over as principal of the Palm Avenue Exceptional Student Center, a facility for the trainable mentally handicapped. She sees in society's attitude toward her students an uncomfortable similarity to the one endured by blacks in the days of segregation: "When I first came

here, the school didn't have a band, a mascot, cheerleaders. There was very little in the way of activities for these kids." Under her guidance, that has changed, and she has placed ever-increasing emphasis on promoting student contributions to the community, hoping that they will help the students gain respect as productive citizens with dignity, rights, and civic responsibilities. As one of the school's publications says, "We walk with our heads held high and that Panther Pride glowing all about us."

Away from her position at Palm Avenue, much of Norman's spare time is dedicated to consolidating the improvements she has seen Florida make in civil rights. Her community involvement ranges from having been director of the Neighborhood Tutoring Program for Disadvantaged Youth to her present membership on the board of directors of the Ritz Theater District, a group working to restore a prominent landmark of Jacksonville's black culture. Her series of letters to the editor on the openness of local drug dealing proved so embarrassing to city officials that they obligingly swept her neighborhood clean. She maintains that if others would get equally involved, a great deal more progress would be seen. "We've got to keep working," she warns. "If we're not careful, we could be right back where we started."

"As a little child I thought the 'colored' water fountain was really supposed to be colored, like colored crayons! I didn't have any reason to drink much water, but I drank because I thought it was going to be colored. I did not associate it with myself. I did not know about colored and white. My father was a very, very fair-skinned man, who could have passed for white, but he wasn't white. And my mother was a brown-complexioned black woman. I grew up in Fairfield, and in Fairfield—it's out where the Gator Bowl is now—there were blacks and whites and foreigners, all living in the same neighborhood. I played with little white kids and little East Indians and some of every other nationality. I was six years old before I found out that I was different, and when I found out was the day that we started school. My playmates didn't know either, because I'm in contact with some of them now and we discuss it. They really didn't know before we found out that we had to go to different schools. They could go about five blocks to the East Jacksonville School, and I had to go way over to Oakland School.

"Then later on—it's really a sad thing—while we were growing up, all of us liked Krystal burgers, and I could not go in the front with them to eat. I could stand there, and they would wait on me and give me the burger, but I had to leave. Well, my friends did not like it and they left with me. I was their friend and they were my friends, but they were caught in the situation just as much as I was. I became defiant one day. I took a seat, and I wasn't gonna get up, and I wasn't gonna leave: I just sat there. And they didn't like it—there were some people who got up and left—and the waitress asked me to get up. But I wouldn't get up. I think I was just so little then, you know, till they didn't want to hurt me, so they didn't bother me. I guess I was about nine or ten, but I was a frail little girl. I felt it was very unfair, and it *was* unfair, and I did what I could in my own way to do something about it. But there wasn't too much at that time that I could do.

"I was on a bus one day—they're talkin' about busing children now, but blacks were always bused, only we had to ride the *city* buses—so I was on the bus, and I saw a poor old black man get on up at Main and Duval, and all the seats were taken, but there was one seat and this man sat down in that seat next to a white man. The bus driver drove about two blocks, then he stopped the bus in the middle of the block, got up, and he came back and he told that man, 'Nigger, what the hell you doin' sittin' next to that white man? Get up!' The man was scared, the man got up, and he stood. So tired— had a little paper bag in his hand. And that stayed in me for a long, long time. It put a certain amount of bitterness in me that I had to deal with from within.

"Because of segregation, there was just nothing for blacks to do, especially children. Everything was totally segregated: the schools, the eating places, and all activities. Blacks were not included. During this time, there was a man, his name was Charles Singleton, but everyone referred to him as Charlie 'Hoss' Singleton. He had a great interest in schoolchildren and he had a great interest in entertainment. He was a talented writer, even back during those days. This was around 1945. He contacted the schools and he got all the black talent to come in and audition. The auditions were at what we called the Center, at State and Broad streets. It was a recreational center for blacks, not very large, but it had an ample floor for practice. There were plenty who thought that they were talented—singers, dancers, comedians—and I happened to go there and audition at the age of eight. I was a dancer, a singer, and I thought I could tell jokes—I thought I was funny. Charlie had had a show before this, but it was not entirely schoolchildren. It was for both youths and adults, but then he turned toward school-age children because there just wasn't anything else for those kids to do. He felt that this way they could get out and show off, you know, and get some recognition. I was a skinny little girl, and I was very, very nervous, but he made me feel comfortable. He was intelligent and kind and interested in youth, very community-oriented. Anyway, I was chosen to be in the show, and eventually I was featured.

"You can't imagine what that did for me, a little girl who wasn't even allowed to sit down in the restaurant and eat a Krystal burger. I just thought I was the greatest thing from here to Alaska, you know. I got to be featured in the show, and I got my name and my picture in the paper. (At that time, even the papers were segregated. They had one page called "News for and about Colored People." I will never forget that.) I was also seen in advertisements which were shown in the black theaters, so I got my picture on the screens of the Strand, the Frolic, the Roosevelt, the Pix, and the Ritz, which we're trying so hard to get renovated into a fine arts center now. I just felt like I was the movie star of Jacksonville! I was very popular with the kids because I was an entertainer, so I just felt a little above certain people. You can see how the attitude that led to segregation can worm its way into anyone's life, especially when they're starved for approval. Kids feel this way, and that was such a great thing to me at the time that being an entertainer became my goal in life.

"We did two shows a year. The April Follies was quite naturally in April, and the Twentieth Century Revue was in September. Charlie had a pianist, his name was Frank Timmons (he's dead now), and he did all the musical arrangements for us. And Charlie had another friend—I think she was a distant cousin or something—who made all the costumes. She was a very talented lady and did not charge much, according to what he would tell us, because all he had to do was get the material. By buying things in bulk, he was able to get it cheap. Remember, now, there was no money behind this. He had to use his own money to get it started and he was just a merchant seaman at that time.

"Charlie would rent the Durkeeville Ball Park on Eighth and Myrtle, which was the right size and location. I think the show was seventy-five cents and it was always a packed audience. It was a big thing for the blacks in Jacksonville. In fact it was just about all they had. They had a restaurant called the Tea Kettle, and they had the Duck's Inn—Alonso Davis was the proprietor. We also would have vaudeville come in from New York, traveling vaudeville. And that would take place, I guess about every four or five months, at the Strand and lasted for a weekend or maybe as long as a week. They would show a movie and then the vaudeville, but it was not something just for children.

"Charlie's show was not entirely made up of children as young as me. Most of the others were about fourteen or fifteen, around that age. Our emcee was a little older: E. J. 'Lawdy' Norman, who became my husband. In fact, E.J. finally went into partnership with Charlie Singleton. Another one of his partners, that served as a choreographer and practiced us, was Calvin Shields; he is the drummer with Red Foxx now. We called him 'Eagle Eye' Shields. Others featured in the show were Frank Mash, Jackie Davis, Frank Legree, Tiny McFashion, Lily Mae Finney, Willie Mae Goodall, Nadine Ponder, Slats Bivins, the ABC Trio (Amanda Miller, Bernice Ship and Camilla Ruff), Charles Lott, who was a very, very splendid singer, and Richard 'Gator' Jones, to name just a few. Some were singers, some were dancers, and some told jokes—sometimes all three. It's just like I told you about myself, my original talent was to dance, but then Charlie discovered that I could sing and then he let me try out at the comedy. He could bring talent out of a person and then he would write material to take advantage of it. I remember a song he adapted for me: 'A Livin' Old Man.' He had me to sing that, but he rearranged it to fit in with a little girl. He was very talented and later went on to New York and became a well-known writer. He wrote 'Strangers in the Night' and the song 'Mama, He Treats Your Daughter Mean,' that Ruth Brown made so popular. (She's now featured in the show *Black and Blue* on Broadway.) Charlie had several hits.

"Anyway, the shows took off and were so popular that we started going out of town to perform. We went to Miami. Liberty City Pool was new then and something for blacks. We appeared there. We went to Savannah, Georgia, and Atlanta, Georgia, and little places in Florida like Palatka and Gainesville. We traveled by automobile and wherever we performed, they'd always furnish us living quarters and food. Whatever they had to offer in the black community, that's where we resided. Sometimes it would be little motels, but often it was private homes, because even if blacks did have motel accommodations, they usually weren't big enough to hold us all. People were generous and opened up their homes, because, you see, we were a big event, and we gave a good show with a great deal of dance. We did tap and soft-shoe routines and jazz dancing and ballroom style, like the samba and rhumba.

"We got so popular that we also started playing a nightclub in Jacksonville called the Two Spot, out on West Forty-fifth Street, a place for blacks to go out and dance, sometimes to bands like Duke Ellington's. Charlie Singleton got a contract out there with Charlie Ed, who was the owner of the Two Spot. We used to have a show out there every Saturday and Sunday night, which brought us in some income. We got paid during that time from fifty to a hundred dollars apiece for each performance, which was a whole lot of money then, especially for young girls and young boys. And we got to share the bill with some excellent performers, like Nat King Cole. That was before he had really been accepted by whites. And we were on a show with Winona 'Mr. Blues' Harris, and with Dinah Washington. And with Count Basie. Of course, he was national, even at that time.

"This was the way many of us got started. We all had role models. Mine was Lena Horne, because she sang and was considered the most beautiful woman by blacks. We thought of her as whites would think of Elizabeth Taylor. This is what I wanted to be, but I ended up doing differently. You know why? Because Charlie insisted that all of us stay in school. You did not get into the show and then drop out of school, or get a lacking into your classes. You did not do this with him.

"So, I stayed in school and got another role model. Her name was

Mrs. Lucille Coleman. She was a teacher up at Stanton, which was the school I attended in the eleventh grade. Mrs. Coleman was a teacher there, and she was recognized as a distinguished educator, like Miss Mary McLeod Bethune, and got invited to the White House as a special guest. That was something back during that time. She was certainly not a glamor girl like Lena Horne. In fact, they were at the opposite ends of the totem pole. She looked nice, but was plain and dressed appropriately for a schoolteacher. She was a little heavy. But I was so impressed with this lady: her mannerisms, the way she treated people, her kindness. She was one of the kindest ladies I have ever known. I loved to hear her talk, I loved to see her walk, I loved the way she carried herself.

"She took an interest in me, as she did in all the girls. She would take the time to talk to me (even after school hours if I wanted to) about my future and my plans. She made me really understand myself. Was I impressed with the glitter of show business? Was that really what I wanted? She told me, 'Whatever you really desire in life, this is what you must achieve. But do you really desire this?' She'd give me things like that, and I'd go think about them. And I was not the only one she did that with. My friend, Harriet Moore, who danced with me in the show, she ended up in education over in Alaska. I liked what Mrs. Coleman was doing for children and young people. Then I dropped Lena Horne, and I felt like I wanted to be like this teacher. So this is how I happen to be where I am now. This shaped my life.

"She directed me away from show business, because, you see, show business is hard. I could go so far with Charlie, and then I'd have to get out on my own to make it on to the top. It is *not* easy to get there. It wasn't a matter of you just go on and someone recognizes you and it's done. It wasn't that way. Going that way, there is no telling how I would have turned out. It could have been disastrous. But this fine lady was such an example until I just wanted to go as high as I could in education, and I eventually completed my doctorate degree.

"Now, I'm in a position to do something like she did. My students are not exactly like hers and instead of having to deal with segregation, we have to deal with things like crack cocaine, but the kindness and individual attention are just as important, maybe more. For example, one of my students has a handicap and he lives in a home where it's deplorable. No human being would want to live there, but he has no choice. The father's sick, the mother's sick. The boy had nothing, but he is a very talented young man, very talented. He can sing, he can dance, he can play musical instruments. But on the streets he met up with the wrong kind of people, and they bought him a bicycle, a very expensive bicycle. And he was riding around sighting out the cops for the crack dealers, and even passing it out himself, selling it. Before they started using the youngsters, they did this themselves, riding up in their cars and Jeeps. But since the law got onto that, they started using these kids riding around on their bicycles, going and coming from school, and they can spot cops, and they are provided with beepers, and they beep the pusher and let the pusher know to beware. And that's what this boy had gotten into. It was terrible, but through counseling and people who really cared pushing his talent, he was able to change. A staff member cared enough about him to start taking him to church, letting him meet the young people who attend church and see the kind of life they were living, to let him know what was possible. And the staff member started going to his home and getting other aid to go in and help this family that needed it so very badly. Now, to my knowledge this boy is not involved anymore. The bicycle is gone and the beeper is gone.

"Individual attention does work. If these kids had a role model and someone who really cared, I think it would really help. In the homes that some of these kids come from, the parents are hooked on drugs. Some of the parents are putting their kids out there to follow in their footsteps. It's all in the home, it's all they see, they're raised this way. So I think if someone just takes an interest in them, it would make a whole lot of difference. We can't wait around for help from higher up, for somebody with magic. Everybody says we lack leadership, but nothing gets done while we're sitting around waiting for a leader. We've got to do it ourselves. There are so many more opportunities now than there were when I was coming up, but young people have to be encouraged to take advantage of them, instead of going for the quick money, which can lead to disaster. That little bit of encouragement can make all the difference. It made all the difference to me."

—*Interview by John Ames*

Burt Reynolds

ONE OF THE THINGS THAT distinguishes Burt Reynolds from most other film personalities of similar magnitude is his steadfast refusal to abandon his home state. In the course of a career that has spanned three decades, he has maintained a home in Florida and as often as possible has brought entertainment productions there. Long before Florida's current filmmaking boom was precipitated by the construction of extensive production facilities in Orlando, Reynolds made *Stick* and *Smokey and the Bandit II* entirely in Florida, as well as parts of several other movies. He also established the Burt Reynolds Dinner Theater near his home in Jupiter as a place where he and his friends could work onstage. In the late 1980s, he created the character of Palm Beach detective B. L. Stryker, featured in a series of network television movies produced in the south Florida area. Even in productions not filmed in Florida, Reynolds has often managed to include affectionate references to his home state. In *Nickelodeon*, his character hails from Sopchoppy, Florida, and in other films he may be seen wearing sweatshirts from Florida State University, where he played football.

This loyalty stems from Reynolds's sense of how much the state

Photo by Tony Esparza

has contributed to his life. Certainly his childhood environment is greatly responsible for shaping a screen personality that audiences have taken to heart. His most applauded roles are athletic, uncomplicatedly masculine, and full of locker-room humor. Reynold speaks affectionately of the good old boys from whom he absorbed these characteristics, when, as a youth, he frequented Florida's back country and its rural bars.

But there is another aspect of his personality displayed in less well known films such as *The End* and *Starting Over*: a sensitive and vulnerable version of the rollicking good old boy that made him a bankable star. The origins of this variation can also be seen in his Florida background, revealed in his unabashed emphasis on the sheer romanticism of the environment that shaped him. He arrived as a little boy of five, found a place that he immediately identified as paradise, and to this day, still uses words like "magical" and "thrilling" in his descriptions of the state. After reading them, no one should be surprised to learn that he is a lover of poetry and an ardent conservationist.

"One of the big disappointments for me," Reynolds says, "is when you meet someone that you like and respect and think is very intelligent, and they think that Florida is just Miami. Or Florida is just the Everglades. Or *just* something else. I'm really disappointed in them. It isn't fair. There's a whole—well, you have to go through this big long speech." Like the state he loves, Burt Reynolds has often been thoughtlessly classified, but after a lifetime of trying, he is still willing to make one more attempt to set the record straight.

"I CAME TO FLORIDA WHEN I was about five years old, and I always felt cheated that I wasn't born here. My father came down on a second honeymoon and he fell in love with the place. He came back and got us, not my sister, just me. She wanted to be with her friends and refused to come, so they let her stay up there and finish junior high school. She came on down in the tenth or eleventh grade, but she came down in the summer, which was a big mistake! When she arrived, she got out of the car and said, 'I'm in hell!' She hated it. I thought the opposite. I loved it immediately. It could never get too hot for me. It could never get too humid. In fact, I like it better in the summer, because there's less people and it reminds me of when I was growing up.

"When I arrived in the early forties, it was an amazing thing—nowadays it sounds like you're making a joke—but there were no houses down by the water. I used to walk along Riviera Beach and see probably the same sights as the barefoot mailman saw. There was even a tribe of Seminole Indians living by the beach, set up in a grove of Australian pines. I used to play with them. One thing I remember in particular is that the mosquitoes used to eat me up, but they never bothered those Seminoles. From the very beginning, there wasn't anything in Florida that wasn't paradise to me, even the mosquitoes. They bothered me, but they didn't bother me.

"I had a friend named Sally, who we called Sally Seminole, which is rather negative, but we did it. She was terrific, and when I was about eleven or twelve, she came to the house and brought a shirt for me. I don't know where she got the money or how she got the shirt, but I was very touched by it; so was my father. I tried to reciprocate and give her a gift, but she didn't want a gift. She said, 'That's not the reason I gave you the shirt.' I was very hurt by the fact that the Seminoles didn't go to school after that. It was about the sixth or seventh grade and they just dropped out, probably because they were kidded so much and took a lot of abuse in school. I never saw them again. I don't even know what happened to them. The families that lived down near the water were, of course, moved on out. Homes were put there. I remember the Sun Dance they would have every year. You could ride through the Everglades and never see an Indian, then on the day of the Sun Dance they'd all start walking out of the Everglades like it was some magical thing. Now, of course, they're on reservations.

"People don't believe this, but I actually went barefooted to school until the eighth grade. Not because I didn't have shoes, but because most of the guys went barefooted with their pants rolled up, and that was the outfit. I used to hide my shoes behind a palmetto bush, so that I would be like everybody else, and I'd pick them up on the way home. My father was very impressed with how *well* I took care of my shoes. But none of the boys wore shoes. Well, maybe one or two guys wore shoes, but we didn't even talk to them.

64   Jupiter

"I first went to school in Lake Park, which was then called Kelsey City, for a man named Kelsey who was going to build this big city but was killed in a famous murder down in the Bahamas or someplace. Anyway, he had built this beautiful school and there was nobody in it. We had the sixth, seventh, and eighth grades all in the same classroom. There were only nine kids in my eighth-grade class and that's why we were transferred out of there. I was transferred down to West Palm Beach, which I was very unhappy about. I had to take a school bus, and it was a long ride, too, like an hour or something. We had to get up at six and schlep all the way down to West Palm Beach. And I had to wear shoes. I hated it.

"I hadn't had much of a sense of community up north and maybe that's why I just jumped at the chance to have some in Florida. Up there, we lived way out in the country. We had no electricity, no radio, and of course there was no television. Also, I didn't have anybody to play with. My sister was six years older than me, and there was nobody else around except for a couple of cows. I played by myself all the time. My mother said she could just stick me outdoors and I would be happy, and I would imagine all these things. I was happy as far as she was concerned, but I was probably miserable, because when we came to Florida, I found playmates quickly, and I just thought I was in paradise. Totally enchanted with it. And I was grateful. I never stopped being grateful. I mean, my feet were warm! Even though I was born in Michigan and spent my first five years in the North, I always hated the cold, just hated it!

"My father was the chief of police in Riviera Beach, and when your father's the chief of police or I guess a preacher, you're either a perfect gentleman or a rebel. I was a rebel. I was constantly being arrested for speeding and always in trouble, but not by today's standards—by fifties standards. That meant I got stopped for speeding twice and probably drank a couple of beers. By today's standards I *was* a perfect gentleman. But in those days it was seen to be wild. It always seemed to be a good idea to me to be going fast, wherever I was going. I liked to speed around, especially in a convertible, but in those days you could. There were very few people on the road, particularly in the summertime. I remember the stretch from West Palm Beach to Fort Lauderdale. There was nothing! Absolutely nothing. I wore a T-shirt with a pack of cigarettes rolled up in the sleeve.

And then, thank God, I discovered athletics and lettered and moved from the rod side of the street to the jock side of the street. Then I didn't wear a T-shirt anymore, I wore a letter sweater when it was a hundred and ten!

"People say now, 'Well, how in the world did you play football in that kind of weather?' I truly believe that the reason we were able to live through that was that we didn't have air-conditioning. Our cars weren't air-conditioned, our houses weren't air-conditioned, so you didn't walk out of sixty-five-degree perfect weather into temperatures of a hundred-and-whatever on the football field. We left this miserable room where we were dying of heat prostration—if someone had a fan, that was a big deal—drove over in our cars with the windows open, put the uniform on, and went out and played. We really couldn't get much hotter. Actually, it was kind of a relief to leave the locker room, which was stifling, and go out on the field. In those days, they didn't believe in ice or water when you played ball. Now they let them have those things, but it's funny that in my day it was almost unknown for anybody to pass out from the heat. We were just used to it.

"Another aspect of football that has changed since I played is travel. When I was in high school, we played in what was called the Big Ten. Palm Beach was one high school, and we would go all over the state to play. We went to Tampa and to Jacksonville and to Orlando. We would usually spend the night and then come back. Now, there's enough high schools in West Palm Beach alone to play a full schedule. These trips were long treks and it was hot in those old school buses, but the experience gave you the sense of being a citizen of the state.

"I remember Yeehaw Junction as one of my favorite places, because when we stopped at Yeehaw Junction we seemed to be in the middle of nowhere; in fact, it still seems like that. You could look out across the prairie and see all those Brahmas and Brangus and different types of Florida cows. The appearance of the place, all of the elements—the heat—I just loved it. We'd stop there for a drink, and that's where I first met some of those old-time Florida cowboys. You hear people say that Floridians don't have accents, but they've never been to places like Yeehaw Junction, Panama City, Mount Dora.

Those are accents! Wonderful accents. If you go just a little distance into the back country, it's like being a thousand miles away from Miami. I used to have a pretty good ear for accents, and I could tell the difference between Arkansas and Texas and like that, but I never heard anything like those Florida accents.

"I knew a lot of Florida Crackers and I was very attracted to them. You'd go out in the Everglades in the late forties and early fifties and there were maybe three people that had airboats and they were—you know—kinda legends. Then there was Trapper Nelson. He was truly legendary. There's a wonderful story about him, if it's true. He was so handsome that some socialite went out there once and fell in love with him. He married her, moved to Palm Beach for like twelve hours, and went right back out to the woods. When I was in high school, we always used to go see Trapper Nelson, who was a big man. Even today he'd be a big man: about six-four, two-twenty. Huge! Looked like Tarzan. Always wore shorts and no shirt. No shoes, I don't think. He just trapped for a living. And he had rattlesnakes that he milked. He had a swimming hole there and we'd all go in, and literally, there were three alligators in the swimming hole, and he used to say things like, 'It'll help your swimming, help you develop speed and agility.' We would actually swing over them on a rope and drop in the water. He loved kids, loved shocking us, putting us to the Trapper Nelson Test: like swinging out over the alligators or holding a rattlesnake. He was terrific, a nice man. When anybody skipped school, we knew where they were at. He lived in the woods in this tin-roofed typical Florida place. There used to be a lot of 'em. Now there's not many of 'em around. It was on stilts. Eventually, I think the state kind of gave it to him, whatever that's called—homesteader rights or something. There used to be a thing called the Jungle Cruise, which was this boat you got on in West Palm Beach, and part of their whole pitch was that they were gonna end up at Trapper Nelson's, which is how I'm sure the Palm Beach socialite saw him. It's still there, by the way, Trapper Nelson's. It's part of Jonathan Dixon State Park now.

"I've seen photographs of him since then, because I thought maybe that—I mean, in your mind everything is always bigger—but he *was* big! I don't know when he died or how he died. He just looked like one of those guys that never would die. He was probably in his thirties when I first saw him, and I'm sure he lived to be in his sixties. He always looked great. I've always been curious about how he wound up out there. He had a thick dialect and was a native Floridian, I'm sure. He loved it passionately, and he would be spinning around in his grave if he knew what was going on in the state now, all the development.

"He had tremendous charisma. We all used to just end up around him at his feet. He was a storyteller, but they were all true. Not so much stories but adventures about how he caught this alligator, how big that snake was. Probably Trapper Nelson gave us the idea to tackle deer. Anything he said seemed like a real good idea.

"One of my friends had an airboat and one of the things we did that nobody believes to this day was to tackle deer from the airboat. You'd see one, and you'd try to get the airboat up alongside of him, and you'd dive out and grab him and roll in the water, and then of course, he would win. I mean, a deer is a handful! But we were sixteen years old and thought we were immortal. Because of the water it was sort of even for about five minutes, and you could always let them go, but they would cut our legs to ribbons with their hooves. We didn't do this to little does or fawns, of course, but if it was a pretty good-sized deer, it became a real contest. We never hurt a deer or tried to. In fact, they hurt *us,* but it was great fun.

"We also went out with the game preserve guys when they would tag alligators. You don't know the sex of the alligator until you turn him over and actually stick your hand in this hole, and then he gets an erection. I remember doing this all day long, and that evening I went into a bar on the Bee Line Highway and some guy was giving me a hard time. And I said, 'Look, before we get in a fight, I just want you to know that I've been jackin' off alligators all day long. If you still wanna fight me, fine.'

"I was always attracted to places that were a little on the unsavory side. Bars and roadhouses and cowboy Saturday-night joints. You know, it used to be get drunk, get in a fight, and have a good time. That was the schedule. It just sort of seemed like a good thing to do at the time. You gotta remember that nobody took guns and knives out and shot anybody. There weren't any drugs around. (The biggest thing we had going for us was what they called Purple Passion parties, where there was vodka and grape juice in the bath tub, and maybe a few beers.) The fights I got in were sort of Marquis of Queensbury fights, and it all seemed rather fun. But it wasn't fun if you got a hold of one of those big cowboys. They were pretty tough. But nobody ever drew a knife or a gun or any of that stuff, and I had hundreds of fights. The worst that happened was a broken nose. I broke my nose about four times. Other than that, nothing but minor cuts and bruises.

"When I graduated from high school, I was offered several football scholarships, and I was going to go to Miami. In fact I signed a grant in aid. In those days, you could break a grant in aid; you can't now. And I went down there, and it looked like the Fontainebleau Hotel. I was disappointed in that. It didn't look like what I thought a college should look like. I visited some others and I was also disappointed, but when I went to Florida State, it looked like what to me a college should look like. It had ivy, it was red brick, there were hills, it had moss, and it had tradition. It also had fifteen girls for every guy! This was 1954. So I said, 'Yeah, this is where I want to go to school.'

"I got hurt at FSU my second year, so they said, 'Why don't you go to community college, pick up some courses and then come back.' So I did that and got the English literature bug. I was real lucky. I had an English literature teacher named Watson B. Duncan. He is one of those amazing teachers that changes your life. I started out in the back of the room—he was doing Milton's *Paradise Lost*—and by the time he was halfway through the book I was up in the front of the room. We went through the whole Romantic period. When we got to Lord Byron, I thought he was terrific. The guy was an athlete *and* a writer. I was not a great student, but I was a really good student in English literature—I made an A, and I absolutely loved the course. In fact I'd like to take it again. It was thrilling to me. I couldn't wait to get to Duncan's class, and I hated it when it was over. Duncan was such an actor when he taught that I was fascinated, and he was the one that first planted the seed for me to be an actor. I thought he was out of his mind. It was crazy! Why would I want to be an actor? Then he directed a play called *Outward Bound*. Why in the world I ever went to see about it I don't know, but I did, and that was the beginning of my whole acting career. I went to summer stock that same year. But up until college, all through high school, I never was interested, not a drop of it. You couldn't drag me to a play. I guess most people have one teacher in their lives who affects them in that way. I was lucky it was English literature and not shop. Otherwise, I'd be a sheet metal worker now.

"But I was just lucky enough that it was something like that, and I am still to this day interested in literature and books. I read poetry all the time. One of the biggest regrets I have is that I never got my degree, though FSU did give me an honorary doctorate. So now I'm a doctor.

"I read a lot of new poets. I'm just interested in poetry generally. I like T. S. Eliot. I always find something new about T. S. Eliot. I'm a huge Robert Service fan, and I feel very strongly about Robert Frost's 'Road Not Taken.' I have that cut out and pasted on my bathroom wall. What I find interesting about poetry is that you can go away from it for five years or even one year and come back to it and find something new. It's fascinating. I think the intent of the author suddenly becomes clear and you say, 'Why didn't I see that before?'

"I'm very eclectic in terms of reading in general. I'm very content to read everything from the silliest novels, trash, to classics. I love to read, usually at night because I can't go to sleep. I'm a real insomniac. So, I'll read to go to sleep, and in a year I go through a lot of books. And I read a lot of best-sellers, just to find out why. What is it about this book that makes it so popular? I like very much to read books that are suddenly hot on the market. Not just in terms of if it's going to be a motion picture, though that *is* one reason I read. But I had read *Deliverance* long before I ever did the movie. Besides, I'm a big fan of Dickey's poetry.

"Over the years people have been surprised to find out that I like to read, especially poetry, because I've played so many macho roles, and even in this interview I've talked about all that roughhouse when I was younger. It's hard for them to understand how both things can be part of the same personality. I think I got that from my parents. My father's like that. He cries at the damnedest things, yet I've never known a tougher man. Hard. About a lot of things he's very hard. I grew up with a set of rules, and I didn't dare break them or I got my ass kicked. I remember once sassing my mother—I only did it once—when I was fifteen. He hit me and knocked me through the door to a closet underneath a stairway. And all the clothes came down on top of me, so I really couldn't see, but I heard my mother say, 'My God, Burt, you've killed him!' And I heard him say, 'No, I've just put him to sleep.' I never sassed my mother again. Yet this is the same man who, in watching a sensitive scene—well, God knows, he'd never make it through *The Yearling* without tears.

"I remember an incident shortly after he became the chief of police. I was about ten at the time. Apparently the chief before him had been on the take for some situations, and a guy came by and said, 'We're having a bolita game over in a certain section of town, and this is your part of the take,' and he gave my father a paper bag full of money. My dad made about five thousand dollars a year as police chief, and that paper bag had *ten* thousand dollars in it. And he dragged that man out in front of the police station and made him eat the paper bag. I came upon this scene on my way home from school. That sight has always stayed with me: this man eating this money, throwing it up, and my father making him eat it again. That's a strong image.

"My father had to be tough. In Palm Beach the police chief was getting calls like, 'Mrs. Dodge can't get her garage door open.' But Riviera was a tough little town full of a lot of very, very tough people—fishermen, what we called 'mullets.' There were a lot of fights and crime there. I later found out that he went in and took guns away from people and stuff like that, but I didn't know about it then.

"Another aspect of my father's sensitivity is reflected in the fact that I'm probably one of the few kids who ever got to pick his brother. I knew him from school and one day I went home with him, and I could see that he didn't have the best environment to grow up in; in fact it was pretty awful. His mother was drunk and the guy she was living with just batted him around. He was very young to be in that kind of situation. I didn't like it, so one day I said, 'Why don't you come home and live with me?' He thought that was a grand idea, but what was amazing was my parents' attitude. When I said, 'Jimmy's gonna live with us,' my father said, 'Fine.' He went up and stuck his hand in the closet, pushed all my clothes over to one side and said,

'This is your side and this is Jimmy's side. He can stay here as long as he wants to.' So he just moved in. My parents knew about his home life, but I don't think they expected him to stay forever! He did, though, and about ten years later they adopted him formally. The most shocking part about it was that there was not a word of protest from his natural mother. I don't even think she knew he was gone.

"You don't realize you have terrific parents until they do something like that. I don't know what led me to believe that they would accept him in that way. At that age you take everything for granted. I just thought to myself, 'Of course they'll let him live here. He can't live anywhere else.' I suppose I just figured that they would understand the situation in the same way I did. Thinking back on it now, I can see how wonderful a gesture it was, and the graceful way they did it was quite magnificent.

"Examples like that probably account for whatever sensitivity I have. Even if you don't realize it at the time, that stuff seeps in. My appreciation for the state of Florida has also become more conscious over the years. My brother and I were talking about this the other night. I said, 'Why didn't we notice the sunsets when we were kids?' And I guess the reason is that you think you're gonna see 'em forever, so who cares? But I do remember being awed by the sunsets out in the Glades, even as a kid. It seemed like it lasted forever. The sun would go down in that water and reflect, you know? As far as you could see was red. I just don't ever remember seeing anything like that again.

"Of course the state has changed, though I can't imagine not living here—I love it so much. But I am mystified that we have allowed the things to happen that we've allowed to happen. Condominiums are just everywhere. It's a mystery to me that the ocean is as clear as it is. St. Augustine is a joke. When I was a kid, I used to go up there and go into the different places that Flagler had built, the old buildings that didn't cost anything to go in. Now, it seems that there are *more* old buildings that have popped up and it costs a quarter to get in or a dollar or whatever. It has a real carnival atmosphere, which I hate. I must say that I used to not be attracted to the west coast, but now I really love Naples and that area. It reminds me a lot of what it used to be like on the east coast. When I hear about certain counties really being tough about not letting condominiums go up, and I hear all this bitching about it—*I* think it's terrific that they don't let that happen. But I'm afraid the old guard is not going to be able to hold on unless these young people understand that they will lose everything if they don't start being as tough. It can't just be a bunch of eighty-year-old people on the board, screaming about progress. It has to be some of these young Turks that have to take it by the horn and not let it happen. I think the only way that's going to happen is if they maybe look at some photographs and see the way things used to be. Or go to Jupiter Island. Jupiter Island has been kind of left the way it was. There are stretches of road that you can drive down where you can't see the sky: the trees form an archway. It's just thrilling.

"John MacArthur, who my Dad worked for a couple of years, was one of the richest men in the world. He was a cantankerous old guy, but I loved him, and he used to say to me, 'If you want to do something for yourself, buy something on the water, because anything on the water in thirty years or forty years is going to be a treasure.' I took his advice and all of the property that I've ever bought on the water has increased in value tenfold, especially down here. He used to be a huge fan of trees and he wouldn't allow anybody to cut a tree down; you had to build around a tree. As a matter of fact, I remember that there was a huge banyan tree in West Palm Beach. I don't remember what it cost him—it would be prohibitive now—but he moved this banyan tree, because he loved it so much. It was a hundred-and-fifty or two hundred years old. He couldn't take it on the road—it was too big—so he put it on a freighter and brought it up the inland waterway. It's planted now in Palm Beach Gardens where he had a home. Whenever I see that banyan tree, I think, 'Why the heck didn't we do that to all the banyan trees?' I mean, why did we just take it for granted that they were always going to be there? The way these people go in and chop trees down! It makes me crazy.

"When I go around the state, and I see places, there are some towns—not very many anymore—that still look the way it looked when I was growing up. If I really had my druthers (if my wife could stand it) I would probably live in one of those little towns, like Sebastian. But even those are disappearing fast. There's a little town between Tallahassee and Panama City that still looks almost exactly as it did in the fifties. But anything on the water seems to have slowly turned into some sort of tourist attraction. Even where the lady that wrote *The Yearling*—once the movie came out it sort of became a tourist attraction. And that type of thing makes me crazy, but you can't have paradise and not have it be crowded.

"I'm able to move around Florida and enjoy it, but in most places I do have to *keep* moving. There are certain places where it's easier than others. In places like Pahokee and Belle Glade, it's much easier because you've got a fishing hat on and you look a lot like everybody else. And if people do recognize you, they respect the fact that you're just there to fish or hunt, like them. If you're downtown someplace, you're liable to get trapped, and then you can't get out of the shop and all that, but fishermen and hunters and cowboys just have a natural reticence to bother you. They're kind of the same way you are. The reason that they're out in the country is that they want to be by themselves. When I'm out on the ranch, I usually get, 'Did you know John Wayne?' and I say, 'No,' and that's about the end of the show business conversation.

"The people who make a big deal over the fact that I'm an actor are usually tourists. You seem to be fair game in a resort type of situation, but most Floridians have a different attitude, more along the lines of, 'Oh, that's just Burt—one of us.' In Jupiter, for example, I can go shopping and go to Joe's Deli Bar. Perry Como kind of set the trend for that. He made it clear that he just wanted to be 'Old Per',' and everybody got used to treating somebody famous like an ordinary person. He still lives down there and goes fishing every morning and golfing every afternoon. Son of a bitch looks great. He's seventy-eight and looks fifty. But the people down there allow you to just walk around, which I really think is wonderful. They allow Loni to take the baby and go shopping and all that. It's just terrific. Outside of Jupiter there are more problems, but in Jupiter there's no problem at all.

"My recreation tends to be in the remotest places possible. I have a helicopter, so I'm lucky enough to see a lot of Florida that nobody else sees. I'm able to set down in places you can't readily get to any other way. I'm always looking for places that still have that old magic. Crystal River is one. When you fly over the Suwannee these days it looks pretty dreary, but Crystal River is so beautiful. I'm always looking for places like that.

"I used to like the old-time attractions in Florida, before they became so extensively developed. Two that come to mind are Silver Springs and Cypress Gardens, which I first went to back in the forties and fifties. I hate to see what's happened to them. At Silver Springs you go through nine hundred things that you have to shell out money for, and you don't see a spring for two hours. And the same with Cypress Gardens. I hate that. I knew Dick Pope pretty well. Of course, Esther Williams became a real good friend of mine when I went to Hollywood. We used to talk about Cypress Gardens longingly. She loved it there. Of course it's all changed. For me now, the big kick is to go up to Wakulla Springs outside of Tallahassee. It kind of reminds me of what they used to be like. Of all of them, that one seems to have some integrity about it. They also have the biggest gators I've seen. They look very content.

"I'm quite attracted to the Tallahassee area, not just because of the college but because it's such a different look from southern Florida, because of the hills. When you've been raised in southern Florida your whole life, hills get to be a big deal. And I love the moss on the trees. I like the little weather changes up there. Just perfect for me. It doesn't get too cold, just cool. I could probably live there and be happy if I had to move away from Jupiter, which has always been a favorite place of mine, because it seemed such a sleepy little town and sort of untouched. It's changing, but it seems to be changing in the right way.

"I've always considered Florida my home and tried to give a little something back to the state—you know, make movies and television shows here, things that are positive for the economy. It's a place that's been a wonderful influence in my life, and even though my work has taken me away from it for long periods, I've always been comforted by the knowledge that I would be coming back here. Whenever I went off to do a film somewhere, whether I got beat up physically or emotionally—and I often did—the minute that I touched back down in Florida, I felt better. It's been a very healing place for me."

—*Interview by John Ames*

Ross Hooks

IN THE 1960S, THE STATE OF FLORIDA declared the alligator an endangered species and banned all hunting of the reptile except for nuisance alligators by licensed control agents. Under the protection of the Florida Game and Fresh Water Fish Commission the alligator population was revived. Today the state estimates that there are between one and two million gators living in waterways and wetlands. In 1988 the state reopened the hunting of alligators by permit. In 1989, more than 20,000 people applied for the 288 permits issued, and legally harvested 3,097 gators.

Now both the human and the gator populations are growing along Florida's coasts. Condominium complexes, shopping malls, and golf courses are built flush against the boundaries of the Everglades, and in some cases, on landfill in the Glades. One problem this human expansion causes is the intrusion of civilization upon the gator's native turf. To most people living in these communities, however, the alligator is the intruder—upon new parking lots, swimming pool patios, and drainage ditches.

Ross Hooks is a licensed control agent. Despite his love of the outback swamps and marshes, he spends a portion of his time around

Photo by Henry Rowland

the cul-de-sacs and golf courses of Broward County. Distress calls come in twenty-four hours a day, from Fort Lauderdale to Miramar. His job is to remove unwanted gators.

Once Hooks captures a gator with a snare, the animal is hoisted aboard a pickup truck and driven to a building in rural Davie. There, out of the public view, he ends the animal's life with a .22 caliber bullet between the eyes. The corpse is then placed on a stainless steel operating table and expertly skinned with scalpels and knives. Hides go to the state for auctioning; gator meat, a delicacy, is sold to restaurants. For his efforts, Hooks is entitled to most of the proceeds.

"I'm not a bounty hunter," says Hooks. "I'm a public servant performing a public service."

"I WAS BORN IN 1944 and raised around Clermont. Us Hooks go back seven generations in America. Max Hooks, my grandfather, traced the family to 1706 in Burnt Swamp, Carolina. In 1859 the first Hooks came to Florida.

"My ancestors were Florida Crackers. One story is how old-timers used to crack corn to make meal for bread. Another goes back to the cattle drives in Central Florida. The ranchers used to drive the cattle into ports like Jacksonville to load them on ships bound for northern markets. They cracked blacksnake whips over the cattle to keep them in line. The term Blacksnake Crackers was shortened to Whip Crackers and finally Crackers.

"When I was a kid, I remember the rednecks and racial riots. In one, the National Guard set up a machine gun nest at the crossroads of Highways 33 and 50 in Groveland to prevent the Ku Klux Klan from burning out 'Niggertown.' I recall hearing about how the KKK tied a black man to a pine tree stump and burned him to death not far from where we lived. Even my daughter recalls the Klan rallies right here in Davie. The Grand Wizard used to live in Melrose Park. He presided over bonfires. They'd burn crosses on people's property. The whole nine yards. That wasn't so long ago.

"I lived close to Hacienda Village before it got incorporated into Davie. For years, Red Crise was mayor of Hacienda. He ruled over the only town in Florida that operated in the black. Even though it was just a one-mile strip of trailers along Interstate 84 (Alligator Alley), it had twenty-three cops for the hundred and eighty-eight full-time residents. That averaged out to one cop for every four people. The crime rate was low. Money was raised on speeding tickets. After Davie took over, Hacienda went from issuing eighteen hundred tickets a month to twenty. Crise was a character!

"I mentioned Alligator Alley. I live in earshot of it. Interstate Eighty-four connects Naples with Fort Lauderdale, coast to coast. It cuts right through the Everglades. Because the road interferes with the natural drainage, ecosystems were hurt and vegetation north of the road differs slightly from that south of the road. It's taken a terrible environmental toll on the Glades and on wildlife. Panthers continue to be hit and killed along that road. The Automobile Association of America described the road when it was first built as nothing but a 'damn alley through the Everglades with nothing but alligators.' Hence its nickname.

"I recall working on my grandfather's dairy farm, milking cows and selling eggs locally. I had a small pet alligator at the age of eight. I kept it on a leash in the backyard by the marsh. I've been interested in the critters ever since.

"I'm a nuisance alligator control agent, hired by the Florida Game and Fresh Water Fish Commission to remove gators that pose a real or imagined problem to people. I'm not a bounty hunter or a trapper or a poacher or a hunter. I perform a public service for the people of Broward County when I'm not working as a water resource manager.

"I've been with the alligator control program since it started in 1978. Prior to that alligators were all but wiped out by poachers like Edgar Sorenson and Gator Bill, who I knew. Gator Bill poached around the Tamiami Trail and trafficked the hides to outlets in Georgia and New Orleans like Q.C. Plott Hide and Fur Company. Other poachers used to sell the hides to France for leather goods—like these boots I'm wearing.

"Gator poaching got so bad that around 1959 the animals were placed on the endangered species list. In the late 1960s poaching became a federal offense. Today, except for a few hides here and there, illegal gator hunting is a thing of the past. The gators have made a phenomenal comeback.

"Alligators are moving into urban areas or, really, urban areas are moving into gator country. When they become a problem, people call the police and the police call the Florida Game and Fresh Water Fish Commission. There are fifty agents like me who get nuisance complaint forms attached to yellow hide tags, like this one I'm holding. I'm to remove one six-foot-long gator from Janet Desapio's home in Plantation. I'm to skin it out and report the date it is killed, its length, how many pounds of meat I removed, and the number of state seals I posted on the meat packages. This form is a death warrant.

"The state auctions the meat off. At last auction, the average price of a hide was fetching fifteen dollars a foot. So a six-foot gator would bring ninety dollars. There might be fifteen pounds of flesh that would sell for seventy-five dollars. So that six-foot gator would be worth about a hundred and sixty-five dollars to me. Over the past seven years I've caught between six and seven hundred alligators.

"There are different methods of catching alligators. I use a snatch rod during day captures. It looks like a fishing rod and reel with a four-pronged snatch hook on one end. You cast over the gator and catch him by the bone protrusions on his back. You fight him to shore like you would a big fish, tiring him out as you pull. Once he's within reach you set a wire snare and lasso him around the neck and tail. I snug the animal up to a tree so he can't move. I carefully close his snout and tape it shut. That's the dangerous part. I tie his feet behind him and haul him to a truck.

"I don't kill the gator until I get him home. It only infuriates people. Once home, I kill it with a twenty-two revolver with one shot between the eyes.

"When I go out after an alligator at night in my Okeechobee skip-jack, I use a headlight and look for the red of his eyes. Once he's spotted, I stalk him quietly. I cut the engine and paddle. I carry a harpoon attached to a twelve-foot fiberglass pole. When I get to within ten feet of him, I drive that harpoon into the soft fleshy spot in his neck. The harpoon is attached by a parachute cord to a styrofoam buoy. Once hooked, the gator will drag you all around a lake, fighting that buoy.

"As the alligator gets tired, I take a snatch hook and hand-throw it, hooking him by the side. I fight him to the gunwale of the boat and snare his neck with a wire loop. I pull his head to the boat and tape his mouth shut.

"You have to make certain they don't spin around on you. I've been bit that way by some small ones. Once his mouth is taped, I haul him into the boat. The buoyancy of the water, and my running adrenalin, helps me do this.

"I skin the gators out at my house in west Davie. I spreadeagle the animal on the skinning rack after shooting it and bleed it through a hole in the head. I wash down the gator with a mixture of Clorox and bactericide and scrub it from tip of toes to tip of nose.

"I mark the hide where I want to skin it and sterilize a razor-sharp five-inch Browning knife to saw through the thick skin. I cut a straight line up the gator's side, around its feet, and up each leg. I work my way to the jowls, removing fat. Skinning an alligator is a delicate surgical procedure. A single hole in the hide will bring down the price twenty-five percent.

"Sometimes I find strange things in their stomachs. Gators use their teeth mostly to catch and hold things. They don't chew but swallow. In one I found fifteen golf balls. This old gator lived in a lake by a driving range. Other gators ruin golf games by eating the balls as they roll toward the green. A friend of mine found an unopened jar of pickles in another.

"I remove the alligator meat with butcher knives. The meat goes into plastic bags, which I package in five-pound boxes. It's inspected by the state, sealed and frozen. I sell the meat to local French and Cajun-style restaurants. The Miami Lakes Inn, Governor Graham's place, calls me for meat. I also have a wholesale alligator meat business. Depending on how it's prepared, gator meat tastes like veal.

"I also capture frogs: anywhere from three to fifty pounds a night. I get from two-twenty-five to six dollars for a pound of frog meat. And I sell catfish.

"I remember when the Gator Park Bar and Grill called me up and asked me to deliver some fresh gator meat on New Year's Eve some years back. It's a real rednecky juke joint on the Tamiami Trail. When I got there, this Miccosukee Indian shaman named Jesse Tiger saw me. He was full of firewater and started dancing around in bare feet with his rattles. Alligator is a sacred totem. He was blessing me for the coming year so the gators wouldn't get me. Guess it worked.

"Gators can be smart. Like the one whose skull I keep in my living room. It belonged to a fourteen-and-a-half-footer. He got so brave he'd literally come to the boat ramp in Holiday Park while guys were unloading boats and beg for food. It took me more than a year to catch him. Another gator I know of was hooked by the mouth. Its jaws were so strong and devoid of feeling that it worked the hook, straightened it, and spit it out.

"I was once chased by a nine-foot-four-inch crocodile. They're vicious. But the cutest one I caught was a six-foot South American spectacled caiman. It's a near relative of an alligator. Years ago, they sold baby caimans as pets. Often they were released into canals, and there they grew up. I caught this one in the elevator on the second floor of a condominium. The old people who called me were all upset.

"People's opinions differ. One guy asked, 'Why don't you have a nuisance dog remover? The gator doesn't bark or keep me up all night or crap in my yard or dig holes under my fence.'

"But most people, especially retirees from New York who live in gilded high-rises here, have a primeval phobia of alligators. They see them as dragons sunning themselves. Immediately they call the police. These are people who have never seen a tree before. We turn down their requests to kill gators unless they prove they're a nuisance.

"Some gators, of course, *are* a nuisance. I was involved in one attack case. A boy was visiting his grandparents in Century Village in Boca Raton. A gator that lived near there was being fed, illegally, by the residents.

"The little boy came along to catch minnows in the canal with an orange bucket. The gator, I think, had to compete with ducks there for food. The feet of ducks are orange. He may have mistook the bucket for feet and lunged for the boy, grabbing his arm. The boy screamed and was released but to this day, he has not recovered full use of his arm. There were lawsuits galore.

"I was called in to hunt that gator. It was killed on sight by a wildlife officer, and I skinned it out. It was a classic example of an alligator that had been fed and lost its fear.

"One old man lived in a trailer park built around a fifty-acre rock pit in Davie. For twenty years he'd leave work from the Seven-Eleven store and buy himself dinner at Kentucky Fried Chicken. Every day, on the way home, he'd feed it to Julius Caesar, a fat, nine-foot-long alligator that lived in a lake by his house. He said it was Julius Caesar 'because everything I throw Julius it seizes.'

"Well, the gator began to crawl right up on the lawn and beg for food at the back doors of the trailers. Neighbors complained and I was called in. When I got there, it was nowhere to be seen. The old man told me to wait a minute. He disappeared into the trailer and returned with a frying pan and spoon. He'd been banging on it twenty years, I guess, 'cause that old gator came across that lake like a shot when he heard it. It stopped within four feet of us and then set there waiting to be fed. I just threw a snare over his head.

"The old man loved the alligator and asked if I was going to kill him. Now, the complaint for that gator was a death warrant, but I'll let you in on a little secret. *That* gator didn't get destroyed. I had a friend of mine haul him out to Big Cypress Swamp, where he was released. The old man was some relieved to hear that. Things like that make this job endearing."

—*Interview by William Pohl*

Photo by Henry Rowland

Louise Gopher

AS DIRECTOR OF CULTURAL EDUCATION for the Seminole Tribes of Florida, Louise Gopher struggles daily with the task of preserving the fast-disappearing Seminole heritage. Her adversaries are Florida's growth and, ironically, the Seminole Tribe's recent success in adapting to it. Long independent and traditionally accustomed to living in small family units, only in the past two decades has the tribe become a coherent force in its own interests. An improved business sense has resulted in greater exploitation of reservation lands, including conventional ventures such as cattle and citrus, as well as unconventional ones such as Seminole bingo, a form of gambling possible because reservations are not bound by state gaming prohibitions. The tribe has also moved beyond selling trinkets to tourists and is now involved in hotel management, with plans to open a full-scale resort in the coming years. Such success in the modern arena has brought a great many advantages to the Seminoles, but it has further endangered their cultural integrity.

Still a relatively young woman, Louise Gopher has seen firsthand the changes in the Seminole people. She herself began life in a traditional setting, living in an outdoor camp, speaking only her

Photo by Henry Rowland

native language, and seldom seeing a white person. Among her other duties, she now oversees the cultural instruction of Seminole children, most of whom speak only English and would rather be watching television than studying their heritage. By an odd twist of fate, this development comes at a time when Florida's white population has awakened to the unique culture in its midst. Louise Gopher is flooded with so many requests from schools and other organizations for cultural demonstrations that she cannot satisfy them all. Thus, for many Seminoles their culture has become much more something that they occasionally demonstrate than it is something that they practice on a daily basis. Still, the Seminoles have shown themselves tenacious, practical survivors, and though Louise Gopher is reluctant to guess about what lies in the future for Seminole culture, it is certain that something of their staunch character will survive in modern times.

"I think," says Louise Gopher, "one of the things that is characteristic of Seminoles is their individuality. Chairman James Billy encourages people to finish education—go to college or get their training, go work somewhere, and then come back and work for your tribe. He doesn't want you just to stay on the reservation. He says, 'We're all for you comin' back to the reservation and helpin' your tribe, but go out and get some experience first. Learn what it's like and then come back.'"

"When a Seminole child is born, they're taken to an older person—man or woman—and that person gives them a name, and gives a little story with it. The name is just a word, like mine means 'to hold.' It's not anything real pretty, like 'Sunshine' or this kind of stuff you read in the books. My daughter's name means 'to get there.' Nothin' glamorous about that. When my son was born, he was named 'to hide' in the Miccosukee language. Josie Billie named him and gave a little story about the Seminole Wars and how we survived by hiding, and he kept saying 'hiding,' and then finally he said, 'This is what we will name him.'

"Our non-Indian names came about as a convenience for the white man. Back then, you just picked out a name white men could pronounce, maybe something from nature or the name of a friend. I think that's what happened, because my grandfather on my father's side—I don't know how many brothers he had, but they all had different last names. One was Oscar Hall, one was Charlie Micco. My grandfather's name was Sam Jones, and he had another brother named Frank Shore. But now we use the white man's way. My father's last name was Jones, and I was a Jones until I married a Gopher. That's how come I became a Gopher.

"I recall the first home or first family livin' that I ever had was in the early fifties in a camp with chickees and the traditional way of life. We were up at Fort Pierce area. It's west St. Lucie County, almost Okeechobee County, kinda where the borderline is. Back then families lived together. I guess it was Mother's side of the family. All the brothers and sisters—my aunts and uncles—they were all in one camp or they were very close by. There were probably four or five families livin' in our camp. This has been the way Seminoles have lived traditionally, in small groups organized around the family. It was convenient in a way, because you had one central place to eat—everybody cooked over the campfire, and they all put their food on the table, and when everybody said come eat, we all came and eat. We had a hand-crank pump for water, and if we didn't have that, sometimes we'd just have a hole dug in the ground, and they'd put a piece of board or something over it to keep the insects and whatever out. They had it dug deep enough that the water would just filter in, and you'd just dip it out with a bucket. Since we had no electricity, by dark time everybody went to bed and then got up early.

"As a child, I don't remember having too much to do. Back then, all I did was play, go out in the woods and play. My parents worked a lot all the time. They worked in tomato fields or some kind of farm-type work, and my brother and sister and I stayed home. We had a grandmother that stayed with us, and we were more in her control. She disciplined us, and I know that she taught us how to do bead-work and this kind of stuff. In those days, the grandparents pretty much did the teaching. They taught us the crafts, and they spoke to us in the Indian language all the time, so we learned that. A lot of the legends and the rules—things like that—we learned from the grandmother.

"We have what is called—what is it, a matriarchal society? We have the clan system in our tribe. We have eight clans. I don't know if I can name 'em all, but we have bird clan, panther clan, otter, big town, deer, snake, wind, and—I forget, there's another one—the bear clan. But you can't marry within your clan—it's like marrying your own brother, your own relative. Each child that is born carries the mother's clan. If the marriage should break up or a parent dies, the mother's side of the family takes the child and raises it, and a lot of times the father just goes on his way, and maybe he visits his child now and then. But the woman has always been more the central figure, and the husband was more of a provider or companion. And another thing is that the uncles on the mother's side and the grandmother on the mother's side did a lot of the discipline.

"As far as a discipline, the Seminoles have a way of doin' their discipline, and that is to take a sharp object and leave a scratch on your arm. And the grandmas usually did that. As a child I knew they did it because we were bad or deserved it, but then later on I found out they didn't do it just to be mean. They have to put a little medicine song or some kinda medicine thing behind it. And then in modern times, like today, it's still bein' done, and we find a lot of complaints bein' made to HRS, because it's child abuse. And yet, it was our form of punishment and discipline all these years. It's just a little scratch or mark on your arm, and it, you know, goes away. A lot of times if Grandma couldn't handle you, you were told, 'Wait till your daddy gets home!' Just like in any family. We weren't really that bad. It just felt like we had a lot of free time to play, and what got us into trouble was when the parents didn't know where we had gone or when we were gonna be back or what had happened to us.

"I don't think I went into town very often. My grandmother would always tell us that the white men would steal us. But then on the other hand, we made all these little bracelets to sell to the white man. How were they gonna get to them if we can't see 'em? If we did go into town, we were told to stay in the car. I wasn't so much scared of the white people, but the grown-ups were, so I just thought, 'I better do what they say.'

"Our camp was on private property, and at that time I think it was a family—Scotts family—up in Fort Pierce, and they just allowed the

Indians to live there. It was more a convenience-type thing, because the Indians were moving around quite a bit. A bunch of people could get together and build several chickees, and you'd have a camp made in just a matter of days, so it wasn't that hard to move about. The person that owned the land said that they could live there, so that's where they lived.

"When I started school in 1951, we'd have to walk out to the road, get on the bus, and go about thirty miles into Fort Pierce to go to school. And I went not knowin' a word of English. My brother and sister had already started, so they knew a little bit. When they had started, they were a little bit older. I mean they didn't start like at six years old, and it was kinda hard on them, but I started at the right age.

"In camp I would usually wear a little dress, and it would be like a one-piece dress with a long skirt, and then it would be just tied in back. It wouldn't have a zipper or a button or anything. It looked a lot like what people associate with Seminoles, bands of many colors. Then when we went to school, we wore what the other kids were wearin'. I don't think I would've wanted to wear my Indian dress, 'cause I would've stood out then. I just figured I'd better wear what everyone else was wearing, so that's what I wore.

"As I look back now, it appears to me that education was very important to my parents. I don't know how the other Indian children were treated or how their parents reacted to their having to go to school, but *my* parents sent us to school, and they didn't seem worried at all that I was going to school—a strange world—and I didn't even know how to speak the English. They just sent me, and I went. They had done the same thing with my brother and sister. And a lot of times, if there was a little activity after school or whatever, my parents would get off work and come. Or if I needed anything special, they got it for me, so education was always very important or seemed very important to them. I'm sure they were a little apprehensive about sending us to school like that, but they were also trusting that we were going to be taken care of.

"And as far as going to school, I don't remember being scared or apprehensive. I think I was pretty excited. I didn't realize what I was gettin' into! Like I said, I didn't speak any English. I remember learning a few words at a time and thinking, 'Oh yeah! That word c-a-n: that meant *can* the other day.' It filtered in, I guess, and I often think if they had all these special classes and advanced classes and remedial classes that they do today, they would've probably stuck me *below* remedial, 'cause I didn't know none of that stuff. Back in those days, everybody just was one class: same class, same teacher, same subject. And that's what I learned.

"I think I had a working knowledge of English within the school year. Since that's all I heard all day long, was English, I had to pick it up. I remember I didn't know how to do my math, though. I didn't know my addition until I was in the second grade, when the teacher said to the class, 'You're gonna stay after school if you can't do this.' And I thought, 'Oh my gosh, and I live so far from town, too!' It sorta went in that day. I learned how to do my addition and simple math. They may have concentrated on my reading and speaking ability in the first grade and that's how come I didn't catch onto the math.

"I never remember having any problems in school because I was different. I remember one little girl was stealing things from my desk or something like that, and I told my dad, and he went and talked to the teacher. And we got moved away from one another, I think. But that's the only problem I can recall and it didn't have anything to do with being an Indian.

"If that kinda problem was gonna happen, I guess it would've happened to me because my family was one of the only ones sending their kids to an all-white school. The rest of the Indian kids—if they were going to school, they were probably going to Okeechobee where there was a lot of Indian kids going. For me and my brother and sister, it was three Indian kids in an all-white school most of the time. But we started school in the first grade with a group of kids, and we just went all through school with 'em, even in junior high and high school. We weren't anything different to them. They accepted us. They never did treat us any different. They'd ask us every now and then somethin' about our culture if they were interested, but not a big issue was made of it.

"When I started school, we lived about thirty, forty miles outside Fort Pierce, almost on the county line, but as my dad got other jobs, he went from working in the farms to driving bulldozers and doin' heavy construction work, and our family gave up living in a camp and moved closer into town. This was also again on somebody's property, where they gave us a little house to live in. I think the rest of the family had moved over here to the reservation. At that time we were all in school, and maybe my father didn't want to move us, so we stayed in Fort Pierce.

"My father did have problems with people wantin' to come into our house to televise us and make a big issue, and he didn't like that. He thought it was very private. His attitude was, 'I'm raising my family just like you're raising your family, and I don't want to make a big issue out of it.' He would never allow any publicity made of our home. I was too young to understand what their intentions were. Maybe they wanted to be helpful or maybe they just thought we would be something interesting to show, but he just never would. I have a friend, Mrs. Williams; she's a historian and she's been a college professor over at Indian River Community College (she's retired from there), and when we were staying on her property, the newspaper reporters would contact her, and she'd ask my father and he'd say, 'No.' Then they would hassle her and say, 'Well, they're *your* Indians.' These were adults talking! And she'd say, 'No, they're not! He said no, and that's all there is to it.' In a way, she was the barrier that kept people from bothering us."

"I believe my dad had what you call the American Dream, because, you know, he was a workaholic. He had to work all the time! Even after he got too old and didn't work, he got up and went out to the pastures to look at his cows, just like somebody had a stop clock on him to make sure he was on time. He just thought about work and doin' something all the time, and he wanted us educated so that we could better ourselves.

"When we were younger we did typical family-type things—my dad used to take us to movies in town—and then we would also go to tribal things here on the Brighton reservation. Back then Field Day was more like a picnic day where they had barbecues and different relay races and stuff like that. We've done it now for more than fifty years, but over time we've made it a way of sharing our culture by giving demonstrations and having Seminole food and so on. We have a traditional camp set up and the people sit out there and do beadwork and other crafts. Nowadays we have mostly entertainment-type things and a lot of tourists come.

"When I used to come to Field Day as a child, I never thought that someday I'd be one of the people in charge of organizing it. That happened because about seven or eight years ago the tribal council realized that our native language was being lost and established a cultural education program, and I got the job as director of the program.

"The world isn't like it was when I was young, and you could grow up and hardly hear any English for the first few years of your life. Nowadays a lot of us speak a mixture. We'll start something in English and finish it in our native language. It's hard for a lot of us just to speak completely English. That's the way I speak at home. I speak a lot of native language at home, so my kids understand it, but I do mix it up. There are a lot of times that I have wanted to say something, and it was so much easier to say it and be more understood if I said it in Indian, but the same goes for English. Some things come across better in English.

"We have a cultural education program on four reservations, and we have people that are assigned to develop materials, and some to teach, and my job pretty much is to stay in touch with these people and sorta work out any problems that they might run into. And I find that each reservation is different. Just 'cause we're all Seminole reservations doesn't mean we're all the same. Hollywood is sittin' in a metropolitan area with the turnpike runnin' right through the reservation, and they have a hard time holdin' onto their culture, because they're right in town, and they have to compete against the gym next door and video places down the street. In Hollywood, we concentrate on the young kids—like Head Start and nursery—that we talk to and teach every day. Big Cypress for a long time had more hold on their culture. They spoke the language a lot at home. A lot of kids just spoke the native language to each other, but I think in the last few years, they may be losing it, too.

"And the program is on a voluntary basis—that's made it hard. The kids are gonna find something better to do than come to class and be given more education when they've already been in school all day. Over here in Brighton, we've always done pretty good. We reach a certain age group, like kindergarten to about junior high school. After they reach that age, they go somewhere else and do other things. Each reservation is different, so I kinda have to go out and visit. A lot of my job is not even so much cultural programs anymore, but I find myself doing a lot of public-relations-type things for the tribe, more or less educating the public, because, you know, they think we're livin' in teepees and rasslin' alligators or somethin', which is a wrong perception of the tribe—what the Seminole people is like.

"Trying to preserve a culture in the modern world is very hard with so many distractions. Something that we still have in common is the Green Corn Festival, which is in June or July, and it's a closed activity, just for the tribal Seminole people. Non-Indians come in, but they're supposed to be invited in by an Indian person. It has so far stayed pretty much just strictly Indians. We have three Green Corn Festivals in the state of Florida. We have ours up around Fort Drum area on a private land, and then I think the people down on Tamiami Trail have two—two different ones—and they're a lot more strict than we are; they probably wouldn't let a non-Indian in. This is one of the cultural activities that the young people really enjoy.

"It's like a New Year's, because it's the beginning of a new year for us. You go out there and stay for about four or five days, however you want. It's really for four days, but if you want to come early, you can. Each day has a meaning. The first two days—I forget what the names are—but it's like the first two days are fun. Just gettin' together, dancing, and that type of thing, but as you get into the third day, it's more serious, more like a religious thing.

"On the third and fourth days, most people wear something traditional. The women wear their long dresses and the men wear shirts and stuff. For a while there, we were gettin' lax on it, and the chairman had me take a whole bunch of long shirts and big shirts out to the Corn Dance, 'cause we had guys who would come, and, well, they didn't have anything proper to wear I guess is the way you'd say it—they'd have T-shirts, shorts, and stuff like that. I got the word out that I had these shirts that they could borrow, and they came by and tried them on—I don't know if I got 'em all back, but I got most of 'em back—and from there on, it sort of stuck in their head that they needed to wear the right clothes to these things. And they'd either bring their own, or they'd come borrow from me again, so whether I want to or not, they come by my house or my chickee to borrow their shirts.

"The third day of the festival is an all-day feast, and then the fourth day the men take the medicine, and there's fasting all day: they don't eat all day and they don't eat all night. They dance all night on the fourth night, and that's when the men scratch with the needles—spill blood—I guess to start a new year. They have certain Indian medicines they take—well, I don't really know that much about it, 'cause the women aren't allowed out there. Then, the morning of the fifth day they finally get to eat. The women and the children can eat in the evening of the fourth day.

"The Green Corn Festival is when our young men at the age of maybe twelve, eleven—somewhere around there—receive a new name. The name that they got at birth is their baby name, and then when they reach a certain age they get their man's name. And this is what we do at midnight of the last night, name our boys. This is very important to us.

"When a boy gets to be thirteen or fourteen, the family usually chooses the name. You have to run around and ask, and a lot of times you'll find that a name's already been taken. Some people with a great memory will say, 'No, you can't have that name. That's so-and-so's name.' It takes some planning. You have to decide long before Green Corn Dance time that 'I have a son that's gonna be a certain age, and I have to get him ready.' And you have to go talk to different elderly people, and they'll suggest some names to you, and tell you things like, 'He died a long time ago and he used to do this and that.'

"And then there are certain rituals the boy has to go through. He has to fast with the men. It's kind of hard on 'em because they're used to eating at the evening hour with the women and the children, and all of a sudden they have to go through the rest of the night without eating, so we have to get 'em ready for that. My brother helped my son through it. That's traditionally the uncle's role. He got the name for him, too.

"It was funny, because not too long after my son got his new name, he was talkin' on the phone to somebody and I heard him say his new name, and I thought, 'What did he say that for?' So I asked him after he hung up, 'Who were you talkin' to?' And he said it was my aunt (she's an older lady) and I thought maybe she asked him, 'What's your new name?' or 'I've forgotten your new name.' I didn't say any more about it, but I saw her later, and I said, 'What was y'all talkin' about? I heard him sayin' what his new name was.'

"She says, 'He was askin' for Danny [that's one of his buddies] and I was talkin' to him, but I didn't know who I was talkin' to.' So she said finally, 'Who is this anyway?' And he popped back with his new Indian name, and she said that she just cracked up. It's funny because it's more of a formal name. If I ever decided to call him by his Indian name, I'd still call him by his baby name, because that's what I've always called him. And if I called him by his other name, he'd probably have to stop and think, 'Hey, that's me!'

"I don't think the tradition of the new name is in danger of being lost, because even though it should be done when you're a young teenager, we've got people that are older that have never been named, and they go, 'Hey, I've never been named!' And they go through the rituals with the young boys, too. It's something that the men, I think, want to hold onto. They're proud to have that second name.

"But we're in danger of losing a great deal. Just proving you're an Indian isn't as easy as it used to be. In earlier times, it was easier to get recognized by the tribe as a Seminole, but as you got all these other people, like the Mexicans and the Haitians, and they all look like Indians, there had to be kinda like a card-carryin' Indian! You had to prove that you *were* Indian, because you could have people walk in and ask for medical service, education, or housing—whatever—and they may not even be Indians. So certain guidelines had to be established, and you have to be at least one-quarter Seminole, and you have to have proof. Some grandma, grandpa—somebody—has to sign these papers. It's not just like you can go announce that you're Indian and expect all these privileges. You have to prove it. And then we have some Indians that don't believe that. They think if you're Indian, you're Indian. They don't sign all this stuff, but if you don't do that, you don't get the privileges that go with being a member of the Seminole Tribe.

"And lots of cultural traits that make us special are threatened. For example, eating together has always been very important to us. I remember when my parents were alive and we would get visitors, the first thing you did was, you cooked something for them; you'd feed them. Never cared how many times they ate, you fed 'em. We have a tendency to do that at my house, and we have people who go, 'Oh, I just ate!' And then they get onto their husbands. It might be a white girl married to an Indian, and they go, 'Oh, you just ate, you pig!' And I have to look at 'em and say, 'You know, that's the way they were raised. You always eat at other people's houses.'

"I still make the traditional food at my house: fry bread and sofkee, that's daily-type food. The fry bread is flour and water mixed together in like a dough, and then you fry that. It's something like those elephant ears they sell at carnivals, but it's thicker. You can eat it plain, or put something sweet on it, or put something *in* it—make a sandwich. Sofkee is a drink. I don't know if it's different today from what people drank way back. (I've seen it described more like a stew, but that might be just historians talking.) The way we drink it, it's just a drink. It has no seasoning in it. It might be rice and water cooked together or grits and water or corn and water. But it's a beverage, and we drink it just like you would coffee, tea—whatever. You might put a little bakin' soda in it to get the watery taste out of it. In the old days, they used to burn down a certain type tree. I don't know if it was an oak or what, but then they would dip out the real white ash, and then they would put that in the sofkee for flavoring, but today we use baking soda. The women that go to sell crafts at all these festivals that we have durin' the winter time, a lot of them sell sofkee, and they don't sell it to the white people. They sell it to the Indians, 'cause a lot of people don't get it at home. It's getting so bad that even the Seminoles have to go to festivals to get traditional food.

"We have gotten into a lot of researching. We realize that our older people are dying—there's very few left on this reservation. At Big Cypress, they've got some people they can talk to. We do a lot of interviews, trying to learn the old things that we don't want to lose. We've already lost quite a bit of our culture and much more is threatened. Like at time of death, there's a lot of medicine that they have to use. It's prepared for the family in their grief and is a part of our heritage that almost all our people accept and want, but we always have to go down to Tamiami Trail to get one of their people to come up and do it. They realize we don't have anybody, so they come up. There may be only a couple of people that can handle that kinda situation. They probably have apprentices, but there again it's hard to get the younger generation interested because of all the work that goes along with learning these things.

"I don't know where we'll be in twenty years. Maybe it's just me, but I don't think many people think that far ahead. They just go from day to day, or maybe they might plan a few months ahead. Hopefully in twenty years we will still have our native language or a trace of it. It's just hard to see that far into the future."

—Interview by John Ames

Photo by Henry Rowland

Theofani Koulianos

THEOFANI KOULIANOS CAN TRACE his sponge-diving family back seven generations to the Greek island of Kalymnos. His grandfather was the first of the family to come to the Tarpon Springs area, where he worked on the divers' boats (similar to those described by Koulianos's friend Tasso Karistinos in part 2 of this book). His father was born in Tarpon Springs—and he made certain Koulianos was fluent in both Greek and English.

Although Koulianos was not allowed to work on the boats and was instead encouraged to go to school, he stays close to his family's seafaring roots by maintaining two sponge boats similar to those used by the traditional divers. He also helps to keep sponge diving lore and history alive in his dockside museum, the Spongeorama.

"MY FAMILY AND MY WIFE'S can be traced back seven generations into the Greek sponge-diving industry. They're from Kalymnos in the Aegean Dodecanese islands. In fact, sponge divers can be traced there to the time of Homer in the eighth century B.C.

"Our grandparents immigrated to Key West around 1895. My grandfather was a sponge diver. He later came north to Tarpon Springs with a wave of Greek immigrants.

Photo by Walter Michot

"The Florida sponge-diving industry began in 1849 when native Conchs from Key West found sponges washed ashore after storms. They started diving for them. During the Spanish American War in 1898, because of the fear of warships, the hook boat fleet left Key West and put into Tarpon to sell their sponges. This buoyed the industry.

"John K. Cheyney, a New York investor, came to Tarpon on a land deal. Around 1905 he saw the potential for a sponge industry here and pursued it with John Cocoris, a Greek. Cocoris influenced Cheyney to finance the bringing over of an entire sponge-diving community from Greece starting with his own family. In came divers, sailmakers, boatbuilders, crews—whatever people were needed to support the industry.

"The peak of sponge diving came in the 1930s during the height of the Depression. There were some three hundred diving boats, a hundred sponge hook boats, and smaller vessels like my *Duchess*.

"My grandfather was a businessman at the time. He owned two supply schooners, three diving boats, and a hook boat. He had a hundred men working for him. He hired out crews and Greek divers and some local black deckhands. The Greeks, being ethnics themselves, had experienced prejudice. They were able to work with the blacks and treated them like human beings. There was mutual respect and everyone worked for equal shares. This was unlike the rest of the South.

"To illustrate just how prejudiced Florida was in the 1930s, there is a documented story about a boatload of Greek sponge divers who put into Cedar Key. Some of the Greek spongers went into a bar and talked with the local girls. Some Cedar Key people didn't like it and had the men arrested. They were locked in jail, and that night they were cut down with axes and the jail was set on fire.

"Prejudices last hundreds of years. A black's a nigger, a Greek's a greaser, a Democrat's a liberal, and so on. It's passed down to children through the generations. Of course, that is finally beginning to change here. In 1976 Tarpon Springs was a community of about eight thousand people. Today it has grown to more than twenty thousand. A cornucopia of newcomers are moving in and with them, prejudices are breaking down.

"My grandfather lived and worked in the sponge industry until his death in 1957. My father was born here in 1915, but Granddad wouldn't allow him to work on the boats. It was a hard life and he didn't want him exposed to it. So my father worked in the packing-houses and curio shops. I was born here in 1946. My father told me to become a teacher or lawyer. I wasn't allowed on the boats. Like the Jews, education was a way out for us Greeks.

"In the meantime, the Tarpon sponge industry declined to a hand-ful of divers and boats. The U.S. government was here. Military bases dumped lots of toxic wastes into the sea. The pollution killed the sponge beds. In 1939 a bout of red tide struck. It hit again in the 1970s. Red tide is a fungoid microorganism with neurotoxins that attack the nervous systems of fish and sponges.

"The Greeks in Tarpon Springs were not educated businessmen. They were decent, hardworking people who came into port after a week of diving and lived every day on shore as if it was their last. But they didn't know how to capitalize themselves when times turned bad. They didn't have the experience to import or resell sponges from Greece until times improved. Instead, businesses started to fold and workers were let go. Many of the boats sank for lack of care and money.

"Financiers were another problem for the Greek sponge divers. They charged high interest rates. Supplies were high-priced. By the time a sponger's expenses were paid, there was almost nothing left.

"For centuries the sponge industry has been secretive. No one would pass along secrets of the trade to new generations. Old divers could tell if there were commercial-grade sponges below by heaving the lead to the bottom and looking at the sand and matter that came up. All without electronic devices.

"To this day the locations of those sponge beds remain secrets. There are ten thousand miles of fertile beds out there and six active vessels working the Gulf coast. The glass is half full but the indus-try is dying from lack of competition. Little guys like Tasso have to relearn everything for themselves. There's no financing or help and they have to build their own markets. Most never get beyond the curio shop stage. It's tragic.

"Back when times got hard, my father left with many other Greek

Americans from Tarpon to work in the steel mills of Gary, Indiana. That's where I was raised except for summers here in Tarpon.

"I came back to Tarpon Springs with my wife in 1975. I couldn't stay in Gary. I had an aching desire to get back into the sponge business. My roots were here. I worked at odd jobs. I bought a string of sponges for a hundred and thirty-five dollars from George Billiris off the docks. I was inexperienced and they were, in my opinion, overpriced. I was the new kid on the block and had to pay my dues.

"I set up a little booth and resold those sponges three days each week. The rest of the week, I attended law school in Atlanta, Georgia. I drove to school and back from here.

"Today I own and operate Spongeorama, a museum of sponge history. I also operate a diving show in town. I have two boats that go out sponging: *Duchess* and *Miss Irene*.

"Last year on the *Duchess* a fortuna hit. That's a heavy squall. It took the crew fifteen hours to travel five miles back to port. The wind was blowing the seas twenty feet above the top of the mast. New members of the crew were praying to Saint Nicholas, but the old sea dogs among them knew how to keep the boat into the wind to ride it out. An American-designed vessel might not have made it. Our boat had a broad beam and round belly. Its design had the rough seas of the Aegean in mind. These boats can take a lot of abuse and they will right themselves in knockdowns.

"Tarpon Springs is changing. It's more commercial today since it's become a large shrimping port. But it still retains an old small-town feeling. People know each other and help each other. You can walk the streets at night. I'm glad I returned to my roots. Someday the sponge industry will make a comeback and Florida sponges will be world famous."

—*Interview by William Pohl*

PART TWO

"I'm a transplant . . . I feel like a Floridian, though."

Photo by Henry Rowland

Tasso Karistinos

ON THE GULF OF MEXICO, at the confluence of the Anclote River and its tributary bayous, the weblike nets of shrimp trawlers can be seen, casting shadows on the docks of Tarpon Springs. These vessels dwarf the *Christina*, a sleek and traditional sponge boat owned by Tasso Karistinos, a young first-generation immigrant from Greece who works at the traditional art of diving for sponges.

Sponge diving was once the preeminent industry of Tarpon Springs, in the early 1900s, and indeed can be traced back to the 1840s in Florida, when Bahamian Conchs and Cuban divers moved into the Keys to dive. There they employed the hook method, a pole fifteen to forty feet in length with a sharp hook at the end used to rip sponges from the ocean bottom. A sponge-trading wharf was established in Key West to merchandise the goods.

By the turn of the century, the natural sponge was considered "Gulf coast gold." Sponges were the most valuable resource in the fishing industry, ahead of mullet, red snapper, oysters and sea trout. In 1905 the first Greek diving crews were imported from the Mediterranean to Tarpon Springs. Using rubberized diving suits, the Greeks revolutionized and came to dominate sponge fishing in Florida. In

Photo by Henry Rowland

1908, fifty local spongers joined together to form the Tarpon Springs Sponge Exchange, which became the foremost sponge market in the United States. By the 1930s, 400 to 600 million pounds of sponge were gathered annually in Florida. Tarpon Springs was home port to some two hundred of the graceful boats, and reaped some $4 million in annual trade.

The fleet's success was short-lived, however. Beginning in the 1930s, the sponge industry experienced a series of setbacks caused by a red tide epidemic that infected sponge beds, the disruption of shipping lanes during World War II, and the coup de grace of man-made synthetics.

Today the natural sponge is staging an ecological and commercial comeback, and the Greek culture in Tarpon Springs thrives, as evidenced by the annual Epiphany Day celebration, the Greek Orthodox St. Nicholas Cathedral, old-world cafés, the world-renowned Louis Pappas Restaurant.

"I'VE BEEN DRAWN TOWARD the sea all my life. I was born in 1952 in Avia, Greece. My father was a fisherman who also dived for corals and shells. He gave me my first diving instruction and taught me to unblock my ears to remove pressure. He taught me how to swim.

"I became an electrician on a ship. I jumped ship in 1971. That's how I came to America. While working in New York I heard about the Greeks in Tarpon Springs and came down in 1973. That's how I found the sea again.

"I worked in Tarpon for George Billiris as a cook on his boat for the St. Nicholas Boatline. He dove for sponges. He didn't let me dive right away. Instead he let me take one dive in shallow water. I had five minutes and came up with a six-inch wool sponge. I could recognize sponges underwater. Many corals look like sponges. So George began to let me dive for him. He taught me many things.

"Today I can dive one hundred or two hundred feet with a wetsuit and an air hose. I can stay down up to fifteen minutes. Air comes from a compressor on the boat. I can dive to sixty feet without a suit and stay down two hours. At twenty feet I can stay down all day.

"I remember July 4, 1979. I was with George diving and couldn't find no sponges. Finally we came to a good place with sponges everywhere. I stayed down seven hours collecting them. When I finished there was sponges on the boat everywhere from stem to stern, hanging out to dry. There was no place to stand up. I brought up twelve hundred pieces. They sold for between two and three dollars each. That was a good day.

"You got to believe you can dive. If you're afraid, you can die. And you must know just how much your own body can take. One danger is the bends. It can cripple you. There's no problem going down. I used to hold a fifty-pound rock or lead and sink to the bottom like a bullet. I brace my legs before hitting bottom and get to work. If your body remains level, it takes the pressure evenly as you descend. Blood goes all up into your chest and head. A rope is sent down for you to come up with. When you come up, you follow the bubbles of air. No faster. It gives your body time to decompress. When you feel better, you go up a little more and let out air from your lungs gradually. If you're free-diving, there should be no air in your lungs by the time you reach the surface.

"As you slowly come up to the surface, blood returns to your lower body and the pressure equalizes. If you come up too fast you can get the bends. Even die. Your lungs explode and all your guts come out your eyes, ears, and nose. Nitrogen bubbles can form in your veins and stop blood circulation. Your veins can pop and you can be paralyzed.

"The old-timers who dived in Greece with rocks used to be able to go down with no air hose to two hundred feet. They'd collect one, two, three sponges and return by rope to the boat—fast. They knew no better. If they got the bends they'd be crippled. It was painful.

"To help the pain, the old-timers would bury the unfortunate diver in hot sand on the beach up to his head, ten times a day. Today you go into a decompression chamber.

"I was once down at the bottom, about sixty feet, collecting sponges, when I meet a good friend of mine. He was there doing the same thing. We started shaking hands and talking through our masks. I invited him for some stew on my boat. He told me he'd bring some wine from his. I couldn't stop laughing at his face. It was all blue from the blood and pressure. When we came up, I told him how funny he looked. He told me to carry a mirror next time and check my own face out.

"Once I was diving after groupers at sixty-five feet. I speared maybe fifteen, each weighing twenty pounds. I had them trailing behind me in a net basket. Suddenly this shadow passes below me. I looked up to see a huge hammerhead shark. I got in the same hole of coral as the groupers and waited fifteen minutes. The shark kept circling, came in and grabbed the whole basket of groupers. All I see is dust as he shakes it from side to side, ripping off flesh. I stayed another five minutes and pulled on my rope, signaling danger. I was pulled right up from sixty-five feet. I wasn't thinking about decompression. I was so scared, my hair was standing straight on end when I got on the boat. I didn't get the bends, but it was a foolish thing to do.

"An experienced diver always knows where he is. Air bubbles rise so you always know which way is up. The Gulf Stream off Tarpon flows northeast to southwest. You grab sand from the bottom and release it to find the currents. As you get experience you can tell from coral formations and sea life where you are. You don't need a compass. Only inexperienced divers get vertigo or disoriented or forget where they are. They say the pressure makes them drunk or dizzy. They're just inexperienced.

"When you go sponging you take two other people at least. One man steers the boat. One holds the lifeline or air hose. You only have one diver at a time so there's no danger of getting tangled in each other's lines.

"You may be attached to six hundred feet of line. The man holding that air hose holds the diver's life in his hands. He must constantly watch the line and stay in touch. It's your only communication with the world above. One tug means you want to come up. Two tugs means you need a helper. Three tugs means you found a good sponge area. Lots of tugs means danger, pull me up!

"Danger can come at you from all sides. Once I had an air hose cut by the boat's propeller. Sharks can be dangerous while you're coming up or going down. It's bad to swim on the surface. When you're thrashing around sharks can mistake you for fish in trouble and attack. If you're spearfishing, sharks are attracted by blood and will circle in. Of course, most of the time sharks are no trouble. And if one wants to eat you, it's probably too late to do anything by the time you see it coming for you. They're fast. The only accident I know of was when a diver tempted a barracuda by flagging a piece of fish in front of its mouth. He lost his hand.

"There used to be three hundred sponge boats in Tarpon Springs in the 1930s. It was the sponge capital of the world. There were more spongers here than in Greece. But the red tide killed off the sponges along the coast of Florida in the 1950s and 1970s. Today you have to go to Key West or Apalachicola to find pockets of surviving sponges.

"Another thing putting the spongers out of business are synthetic sponges. And there's the bait shrimpers. They drag the bottom with nets and rollers. They break off the coral and sponges. Life on the bottom is disturbed. They catch fish with the shrimps and kill the food chain. Nobody will do anything about it because a lot of money's involved. Someday, though, all the shrimps will be gone too. Maybe then the sponges will make a comeback.

"Sponges are still sold in Tarpon in gift shops and at the Sponge Exchange, which buys sponges wholesale from all over the world for three dollars. The sponges are resold at up to thirty-eight dollars each. The only way for a guy like me to make a profit is to cut, clean, and bleach sponges myself. I've got my boat now. I'm going to make a go of it and try to make a living."

—Interview by William Pohl

William P. Foster

DR. WILLIAM P. FOSTER is one of the few people you're likely to meet who will dig into a filing cabinet, bring out a sheet of paper containing his philosophy of life, and hand it to you with the comment "It needs some editing." This is the degree of organization and attention to detail to be expected from the man who for more than forty years has shaped the intricate maneuvers of the Florida A&M Marching Band. For most of those years, Floridians have felt a proprietary pride in "The Marching 100," but in recent times have had to get used to the fact that it is now being called "America's Band." This national adoption has come about as the result of an electrifying appearance in France's bicentennial celebration, an appearance that had the skeptical French shouting, "We love the Americans!" No wonder that praise for the Rattler band was promptly placed in the congressional records of both the Senate and the House of Representatives. And it wasn't the first time, either.

Such acclaim is an endless source of delight to Foster, who sees it as an entirely appropriate reaction to a degree of excellence that is solely the product of exhausting labor by him, his staff, and his students. The complicated figures that the band creates, the demand-

Photo by Walter Michot

ing marching and dance steps, and the flamboyant instrument movement all require substantial mental and physical stamina. In addition, A&M's band members must learn all their music by heart and can play more than thirty-five selections from memory.

Though Florida A&M's first band was organized in 1892, it was not until Foster took over in the late forties that the organization began evolving into a powerfully positive force for a school that had long struggled with the inequities of a segregated educational system. Under his direction, Florida A&M's band program has brought the university a renown that has doubtless had a positive effect on everything from state funding to the recruitment of National Achievement Scholars, in which Florida A&M has recently ranked among the top five schools in the nation.

At age seventy, Foster still gives the impression of a man with an endless capacity for working at the refinements that have raised his organization to its present heights. Nobody knows better than he the worth of his accomplishments, and he speaks with matter-of-fact pride of the central role he has played in the development of what has been called "the most imitated band in America." Next to the file folder containing his philosophy of life is one containing a "Listing of Innovations and/or First Performances" attributable to the A&M Band. It is certainly a long list, but the real proof of Foster's accomplishment is not in any statement of philosophy or any listing of innovations, but in the sight and sound of his band, which lifts the spirit and puts a strut in the step.

"I'M A TRANSPLANT . . . I feel like a Floridian, though. I've been here for the last forty-three years, but Kansas City's my hometown. I received my bachelor of music degree from the University of Kansas, and while I was there, I had an experience that in a roundabout way was responsible for bringing me to Florida. In my senior year, some way I had to drop into the dean's office—Dean Swarthout. You've probably heard of Gladys Swarthout? Well, this was her father. Anyway, he asked me what did I wish to do? This was one of the few times I ever received any counsel at the University of Kansas, because at that time, between the races, it was just purely black and white.

You know, just a number. So I told him that I wanted to be a conductor, and the first thing out of his mouth was 'There's no jobs for colored conductors in this country.' That left a stinging impression on me, really for my entire life. After that incident I began to think, really not too consciously, that I would have to go someplace where I could develop my own organization. I knew it would have to be a black band, a black band as fine in musicianship and performance as any white band. At that time there were very few completely black bands that were of any consequence. Even when I came to Florida here, it was . . . pitiful.

"But before I arrived at Florida A&M University in 1946, I worked in music education for five years: two years as the director of the band and choir at Lincoln High School in Springfield, Missouri (they'd hardly even *seen* an instrument there—that's in the Ozarks), then one year as director of the music department at Fort Valley State College in Fort Valley, Georgia, and finally for two years as director of the band and orchestra at Tuskegee Institute in Alabama. The president of Florida A&M saw our band at the football game, and based on that, he offered me a position here. I don't know that the band was that different at that time, but he may have seen that it was well organized and that the music was played well, which was a rarity back in those days, you know, because bands really left much to be desired. Then again, even at that stage of my career, certain things about me were in evidence. I was just a developing musician and band director, but I always had that positive attitude, and I was hungry for knowledge.

"I can give you an example. When I was teaching in Springfield, Missouri, Mr. Edward Peters, a former member of the John Philip Sousa Band, lived in Springfield. The name John Philip Sousa was very intriguing, you know, because Sousa is at the top of the top drawer. Some way, I found out about Mr. Peters, and I asked him if I could study with him. I had a lot of nerve, I guess. He'd just retired and probably hadn't planned on having students, but he became interested as a result of the fact that I wanted to study with him and to obtain knowledge of his varied experiences with the Sousa Band. That's the main thing that I wanted. I didn't realize it at the time, but really that's what it was. And as we went along, he gave tidbits of his experience with Sousa. I really can't recall now just what some of those things were that he passed on to me from Sousa, but I'm pretty certain that I made them part of my inventory. He deepened my appreciation of detail, articulation, and dynamic contrast—basically subtlety and refinement. That's been over forty-some-odd years ago, so it's difficult to recapture the details, except that my working with him is still a part of my life and my development. But that's how I've always been—open to everything, like a sponge.

"So I arrived at Florida A&M and found that there were only about sixteen battered instruments, and there weren't even many students that played instruments. I came near the end of the war, and a number of the students in my first band were veterans; they were older people who had been away from school for three or four years. You've probably heard of Julian 'Cannonball' Adderley? Well, he was in my first band. It consisted of forty-five musicians, which is a small number compared to the two hundred and fifty we have now. But even though our number was small and our equipment below par, we approached everything with that positivity you've got to have if you want to succeed. I sort of pride myself on the fact that so many of my band members have gone on to prominence in other fields. I call it 'transference of learning.' The character, academic attainment, leadership, and willingness to serve are ingredients that helped them succeed. All are attributable to their experiences in the band program.

"The style of the band has been a gradual development. The embryo of it started in my first bands here at Florida A&M. When the students had a good rehearsal, the tempo would go up—there was sort of a joy type of a thing—and, going off the field, sometimes they'd try to make a few fancy steps, and we started having to put that in, in order for the entire section to do it or no one to do it. Same thing with instrument movement. I would say all this came about through the students' desire for diversity and to hold down boredom, and I decided to include it because I noticed that it sort of captured the eye. This is where one has to have perception. We try to not discourage new ideas. We want suggestions to keep coming from the band, because they make many of the suggestions that make it possible for us to have the type of success that we do. What we do with some of those rough stones is that we modify them, polish them and change them around. We may get a bushel basket of suggestions and use something like a pint. You know, kind of crush it down to that kernel, but all the time keeping that creativity coming forward, because you never know when a good idea's going to come. Then what you find is that, with some of those suggestions, they form spin-offs for other things. Very few times do you use the initial suggestion, but still you may have used a spin-off which came from that original suggestion.

"By the mid-fifties, the band had become nationally recognized. It hadn't hit television yet, but—it's just amazing—it was still known throughout the country. To me that's a mystery. Word of mouth is probably the strongest form of PR that you can get. It may surprise you that, because of that recognition, my doctoral dissertation, written in 1955, was accepted with no references. It was most unusual that they would permit anything like that, but they did. The band's reputation allowed the committee to view my dissertation as original and authoritative. Thirteen years later it was published under the title *Band Pageantry*, and it has been the bible for marching band directors for twenty or more years. One unusual thing about that book is that it is just as fresh and pertinent today as it was in 1968 when it was published, because it deals with fundamentals.

"The appearance that really put the stamp of excellence on this band in the popular mind was on the 'All Sports Show' in about 1962 or '63. They had never seen anything like this before. We created an animated basketball player shooting a basketball. So, instead of having a prop for a basketball goal, we had players to do that. Instead of having a round prop for a ball, the saxophone section made the ball. And all these are moving! The basketball player moves his arms upward—remember, these are bandsmen—the ball goes up and around and then we had enough bandsmen to form a goal and a net. That saxophone-section ball goes right on through that net, the net opens up, and then—let's see, did they form . . . ? I think when they ended that, they formed the number two, which would be two points. And the tune that we played on it was 'Sweet Georgia Brown.' So you see, like with the Harlem Globetrotters, everybody just automatically knew what was going on. That relevance plays a big role. The impact comes from the marriage of the music with the formation or the maneuvers on the field. The music fits most of the movement just like a glove. You put that together with a very simple, direct script and you have our basic formula. There's a very strong correlation between those three. Most people don't realize that.

"Animated movements like that basketball player and the flying American eagle we did for Super Bowl Three gave us our first broad national reputation, because it hadn't been done very much. That type of figure has become our signature. We find that even today, there is as much or greater interest as there has ever been in forming animated pictures or designs on the field. They are all still hits! Because it's something that most bands cannot do. Or they can't make them come off, I'll put it that way. In the beginning, I worked them out on paper. That's where my early education came in. In fact, my starting work in this area probably had to do with having taken industrial arts, because I've always liked to make things. You know, you've got to use a ruler and be very precise. I've always liked science, especially geometry and mathematics. It used to take me hours and hours of drawing to perfect a concept. Now our shows are computerized. If you want to form a flower or heart on the field, you just press a button and that whole thing appears! But I'll tell you what, my staff says that some of those early formations I used were so exact that they compare extremely well with those that are now being done with a computer.

"Since that first show, we've been on television regularly, but we've never been seen by so many people as when we went to France to march in their bicentennial parade. Five hundred million people worldwide saw that! How that came about is an interesting but a very short story. I received a call from a person in Miami who said that they were looking for a band in America that was different and might be interested in going to France for the bicentennial. Well, I had never heard of the bicentennial, but I told this person that we'd certainly be interested in thinking about it. So, then the next inquiry I had was from Paris, France. A member of the bicentennial planning staff asked for press materials on the band—articles, pictures and whatnot. I sent those over, and then the next request I got was, 'Do you have a video of the band?' So I sent the video over. Then they indicated they'd like to come to America. They said, 'We wanna see this band,' because when they saw it on tape, that really engaged them.

They wanted to come to the campus, but I told them I didn't think that would be the best means of sighting the band. I said, 'Two weeks after the time that you want to come, we will be in Tampa, Florida, in Tampa Stadium and we'll be presenting a pregame show and a halftime show and be playing music in the stands. The band will be in uniform, and you'll just be able to get a good perception of what this band is.' Well, later on I got word back that that's what they were going to do. So, they sent three or four representatives, including Jean-Paul Goude, who was the artistic director of the parade. Upon leaving the stadium, they indicated that they would hope to see us in Paris. They had already decided.

"So the French government spent five hundred thousand dollars to bring us to France to perform in that parade, and that is all! No other performances. In fact, the other thing that was interesting was that we could perform no other music than the music of James Brown! Jean-Paul Goude said that the music of James Brown and his performances ushered in that era of black music that influenced so much of the world. Well, we had reservations. We had reservations for the reason that we had so much more to give, and the music of James Brown for us at the time was a very minute part of what would show off the ability of the band. But we agreed, and it was only at the parade review that we realized the impact this was going to have. This parade review was when they went through everything in the parade before the parade itself. This review was held from one to five A.M. on Thursday morning. How about that? But thousands of people were out all that morning to look at the parade review, and every time we would strike up with a James Brown tune, they would dance and snap their fingers and whistle. The response was so great that we were moved from seventh in the parade to last position: the closing climax!

"During the parade itself, every time we would strike up, one to two million people went into their act, just like at the review! They had no reservations whatsoever—and these were the elegant French! Now, in general the crowd was very orderly because there were twenty-five thousand policemen out there. The police could literally lock arms to keep people back, there were so many of them. But after we had moved down the parade route, I guess about half a mile, we noticed to our left there was a big surge of people. This was on the Champs-Elysées, and if you're familiar with that street, well, that's a very wide street that can hold a lot of people. I never knew a street was that wide in the world. Anyway, the people were orderly, they weren't threatening to the band, but they broke through the ranks of police and there were hundreds of them on the left-hand side of the band. After another half-mile, I turned around and looked, and as far as the eye could see, it seemed that about a hundred thousand people had formed in behind the band. It looked like a combination of Times Square and the Mardi Gras all mixed in together. There was a feeling of gaiety, just all over.

"The Russian band was not too far ahead of us (there must have been about five hundred of them) and when we disbanded, their director and assistant director came over and said 'Please play!' They'd heard us and wanted some more, so that was the only time we played anything other than James Brown. We played 'When the Saints Go Marching In,' and they just went goo-goo. They indicated that they wished they would be able to do the things we do, but they said the old folks won't let them! In fact, the next day at the huge racetrack where they fed us some of our meals, the Russians assumed the initiative in exchanging T-shirts and jewelry. They couldn't speak English and we couldn't speak Russian, but they made it known they wanted anything American. And they had smiles on their faces. It was jubilation! I couldn't hardly believe my eyes and ears that these were Russians, really.

"And you know something very interesting? In all the news coverage of this band, which described us as sensational and every other superlative you can think of, to my knowledge we were never known as a black band from America, but just as an American band. The French repeated over and over, 'We love the Americans!' And you know, that's unusual for the French! And people from all over the world had the same reaction. It's funny. So many years ago, I started out to form a black band, in order to make an opportunity for myself to develop my talents as a conductor, and now they're calling it America's Band. And I think that's a very healing thing for everybody. It just shows where the search for excellence can lead and what kind of benefits it fosters. We know full well that we'll never reach perfection, whatever we're doing, but that's what we try for. And that's a pretty good philosophy, because it keeps your hatband the same size. You know, I often tell the kids in the band, I've made a downbeat thousands and thousands of times, but I'm still trying to make that perfect downbeat."

—Interview by John Ames

Photo by Walter Michot

DANIA

Edmund Skellings

EDMUND SKELLINGS WAS NAMED Florida's poet laureate in 1980 by Governor Robert Graham. Friends promptly and unofficially dubbed him "Official State Visionary." He is also known as the Electric Poet. The license on his black Eldorado reads "POET 1." He sports a graying ponytail over the collars of well-tailored pin-striped suits, when not dressed in loud Hawaiian shirts and Bermuda shorts. He is gregarious, incorrigible, quick-witted. He values words. So much so that when one hits him just right, it often lofts him into verbal explorations, flights of fancy, and etymological excavations.

Skellings is a self-proclaimed "great reader" of poetry. Indeed, he does have a mellifluous voice, an excellent sense of pacing, an uncanny ability to bring meaning to his own poems and those of others through varying inflections, intonations, and emphases. He is often called upon to speak, read, and lecture at an eclectic assortment of conferences and institutions ranging from the Third Hemisphere Conference to the Gulf Coast Economics Club and the Florida State Poetry Conference.

Born in Ludlow, Massachusetts, in 1932, Skellings cultivated a traditional academic background: prep school in Connecticut's Suf-

Photos by Henry Rowland

field Academy, a B.A. in English from the University of Massachusetts (where in 1957 he was named Class Poet), Ph.D. from the University of Iowa (where he taught in the famous Iowa Writers Workshop). His career has spanned several decades and states from Alaska to Florida.

As his reading skills suggest, Skellings preaches the gospel of the *spoken* word. "Written poetry is meant to be spoken aloud," he says with gusto. True to this conviction, he pioneered in the oral art by enclosing in the jacket cover of one of his early books two long-playing vinyl disks. Called a recordbook, the disks feature him reading the entire book.

An early computer hacker, Skellings immediately fell in love with the first personal computers. He keeps a dusty collection of these early machines in the garage at his Dania home. His experimentation with animated color poetry uses PCs to color and move words according to mood and tempo, hence the Electric Poet title. He is not only copyrighted but patented: I.B.M. published his Electric Literature series, including software with unlikely names like "Dictionary Dog" and "Comma Cat."

Here Skellings ruminates on Florida and closes with a poem. "Everything from the restaurants to a grain of sand is raw material for the poet to examine," he says. "I like to press down upon words until they give up their life and soul."

"THE POET IS THE CONSTANT SYMBOL. Where does the poem happen? It happens in your head. If I run away to Algeria and join the Foreign Legion it will do me no good because I will still be with me, leaning on a rifle, looking at sand dunes. If I run away to Monaco and sit on a yacht sipping champagne, it will still be me looking out. I will have the same sorrows of spirit and joys. No matter where I am or what I'm doing. No matter what the sense impressions that come storming through the five sensory routes. It will still be me processing and interpreting. A poet is a person whose raw materials are himself. The nooks and crannies of his own psyche. Ultimately poetry is extraordinarily private. The poet's requirements are quite simple. He doesn't even need a pencil. I could retire to the beach and write words with my toe in the sand, letting each wave wash each word away.

"Do you remember Archie the Cockroach that Don Marquis wrote about? Archie wrote lovely poetry in the middle of the night by jumping from typewriter key to key when everyone was asleep. He used to say: 'Publishing a book of poems is like throwing rose petals into the Grand Canyon and waiting for the echo.' And, of course, you do wait for the echo. You really do try to hear something after the poem.

"Occasionally one is called forth to read old poems. The poet's job is to read them as if you've just discovered the lines as they were happening in your mouth. If you can do that you'll be a good reader. Robert Frost, who I knew, said: 'No surprise in the writer, no surprise in the reader.' The real surprises, of course, take place as you're attempting to get thoughts on paper. It should surprise you when a poem goes off in your head. Critical mass is reached and a big mushroom cloud ascends. Or, at two in the morning, you see a line at an odd angle and laugh.

"As a young man you want constructive criticism. But not too much. You may want applause. But there comes a point when the poet realizes the poem is not made any better if three thousand people applaud. Nor is it made any worse if eighty editors reject it. It is simply as good as it is. The world around you cannot tell you whether it is good or bad. The fashion of the day has nothing to do with it. You might even find out you are the greatest poet that ever lived . . . posthumously.

"Ben Jonson said: 'He who casts a living line must turn that line and himself with it.' Writing is a feedback process with your own soul and character. That process requires no museums, no symphonies, no outward manifestations of culture. So you can write poetry, even in Florida.

"Florida is not a cultural wasteland. We have, in America, a culture of the material. We don't have cathedrals like those in France. Or our cathedrals are monuments to something else. If you eat in Yesterday's Restaurant in Fort Lauderdale there is culture. The beef wellington is magnificent. The chocolate mousse is marvelous. The salad bar is impeccable. Before the Early Bird Special the service is excellent. And the decor—the little Christmas lights set two inches apart from each other all year 'round—is splendid. It's Versailles, Rome, and Venice. It's culture.

"Here you have a culture of business. As Calvin Coolidge said, 'The business of America is business.' Florida is a business state. It's filled with agribusiness, tourist business, and high-tech business.

"It's also filled with middle America. You get a quick snapshot of what America is like here. It's a short-term profit and greed place. People want to make it and make it *now*. Instantly. We live in an instant society. Not only instant wealth but instant consumption of that wealth. There is an average indebtedness on Mastercards here of about eight hundred dollars a person. Florida contributed to a massive national debt. No one here looks at what we owe back . . . or what we owe forward. There's only *nowness*. Instant living.

"Florida was built in fifteen years. The old New England tradition of 'Go forth, son, and build it right' is replaced here with 'Go forth and take out as much profit as possible on the front end and make sure that if the building collapses, liability is held by somebody else.' Florida lets the future worry about the future.

"We might not like that image of America. We might fight against the *me*-ness of it. But that is the culture here at the moment. I don't say if it's bad or good. Poets don't make value judgments. Not until they're seventy. . . .

"Florida and America are very conformist. Democracy levels everything to the lowest common denominator. To be a radical all you have to do here is grow your hair four inches longer than other people [motioning to his ponytail]. All you have to do is nothing for five months. Your hair will grow and you'll be a radical. America has taken equality to its final resting place.

"What made Florida is jet aircraft and air-conditioning. It means that New York can fly into Miami in two hours and be comfortable. With air-conditioning—freeze-dried air—every place in the world can be the same. Seventy-four degrees. Every bar, office, and bedroom: seventy-four degrees.

- "You must remember Florida absolutely changed itself all at once from a Deep South state to a division of southern North and northern South. All the population came in during the same period. All the architecture is the same. Norman Mailer was sitting with me in the Americana one night and commented how, except for art deco, Miami buildings were like ice cube trays on end. The remark was somehow redolent of air-conditioning and the ice reminds me of all the jewelry everyone wears. All the population came in during the same period.

"Culturally Florida never caught up with itself. A culture like Boston or Paris hasn't had time to develop. And there was no time between buildings for fashion and genre to change. So it's all the same building blocks here.

"There is also a sameness among Florida's retirees. They've fought the Good War and arrived at sixty together. They come down here in the sun to settle down with people who have like opinions on the right and on the left. They retire into similar communities. Everyone's retirement is all laid out by a common formula.

"We've developed, in Florida, an expensive waystation. God's Waiting Room. We load people on jets and bring them down to the air-conditioning and condos. The next stop is the hospital. Then the cemetery. Planners built excellent roads that lead straight from the airport to the condo to the hospital to the cemetery. We're excellent at processing people down here the way we process oranges. And we're getting rich doing it!

"Florida is transient. Touristville. A good cross-section of Nebraska on the way to see Disney World. People are on the way to Puerto Rico. We're a crossroads between two hemispheres. Transience is a nice place to be permanent.

"Travel is an exhibition of a restlessness of spirit. You can be restless in place too, of course. T. S. Eliot once said: 'Teach us to sit still.' But we aren't eastern. We don't sit still and fast, pun intended, and meditate for eight days. We move around. Not content with the present and lacking a past, we, in Florida, look to the future.

"This is a future-oriented state. Secretary of State George Firestone labeled me the Official State Visionary. I'm a poet who works with computers. I used to have nine in my living room. In 1972 I was into electric poetry. I toured fifty universities with a rock band and multimedia light show. I augmented poems using electronics in the microphones. I turned my garage into a discrete quadraphonic recording studio and experimented with poetry. I used computers to color the English language and developed a program for I.B.M. called Electric Poet.

"I'm future oriented. It's no surprise I'm in Florida. Why, this is the only place on earth where you can go to the moon. We've done it:

We are South looking North.
Or vice versa.
We are international
And exceptionally local.

From here you can go to the moon.
And we can prove it.

Even the natives are transients.
Arriving and departing,
We are of two minds.

Coast to coast here means
One hour through our cotton mountains.
The sun rises and sets under salt waters.

Knowing in the bones that space is time,
We are wise as any peninsula.
We mine the dried beds of forgotten seas.
Fresh mango and orange bloom from the silt.

Outside Gainesville once, I reached down
Into time and touched the sabre tooth of a tiger.
No atlas prepared me for the moist
Sweet smell of his old life.

Suddenly a flock of flamingos
Posed a thousand questions,
Blushing like innocence.

But the moon, perfectly above Miami
Like some great town clock, whispers,
'Now . . . yesterdays . . . tomorrows. . .'

And standing tropically and hugely still
At this point of meditation,
Reduced to neither coming nor going,
We are together on the way to somewhere.

In good time."

—Interview by William Pohl

SAWGRASS TERRITORY

George Mercer

AN AIRBOAT APPEARS ON the surface of a canal in the Sawgrass Territory, skimming over algae blooms and lilies, fishtailing into the bends at twenty miles an hour. It's piloted by George Mercer, sitting atop a high leather seat and gripping a joystick. His ears are plugged to protect them from the roar of the engine. Insects smear the outside of his sunglasses. He looks supremely happy.

"Just when you think you know your way around here, the place changes on you," he says. To make his point, he lifts his T-shirt to reveal a scarred chest. Several years ago, his airboat ran amuck on a newly formed mudbar. The impact threw him over the bow, and the boat ran over him, breaking ribs and piercing a lung. Mercer managed to make it out of the swamp, thirty miles west of Fort Lauderdale, and spent the next few months in a hospital.

Mercer cuts the engine in a slough and the rushing of humid air slows to a halt. Removing earplugs, he listens as the sounds of distant bullfrogs and crickets mingle with the buzzing of cicadas. A coot splashes out of sight, and off to the side in a culvert rests a small alligator, watchful eyes piercing the black water.

In his teenage years, Mercer was befriended by an elderly gator

Photo by Royce Mercer

poacher who introduced him to the ways of the swamp. The old poacher squatted in a small shack on a remote moss hammock. There he skinned his prey and hid from the law.

When the old poacher finally retired, Mercer inherited the shack and began to lead a double life. To make ends meet, he worked as a lineman at the Florida Power and Light Company, replacing streetlamp bulbs in Fort Lauderdale. Weekends, he headed for the swamp where, for several decades, he shored his little island using a shovel and wheelbarrow. He planted rows of cypress trees. He added rooms to the shack, which soon became a cabin, and later a two-story surburban-style house, complete with an electric generator, satellite dish and television, and two Florida Power and Light sodium street-lamps, planted into the peat. At night, moths and insects make eerie halos around the lights.

"All you hear out here are the sounds of nature. Rain pattering on the roof, gator grunts, and occasionally raccoons," says Mercer. "What you don't hear are street noises 'cause there's no streets, cars, or sirens. This is one of the few places in the world where I'm truly at peace."

"I WAS BORN NEAR Blakely, Georgia, in 1929 and grew up helpin' my dad with farm chores till I was about seventeen. I came to Florida to work with a company that grew sod in Davie. In 1948 I got a job diggin' pole holes by hand for FPL in Fort Lauderdale. It was back-breaking work but it got me in pretty good shape. I'm still with FPL today. I change streetlight bulbs.

"I got interested in the Glades when I was a kid. This friend of mine had an airboat. He asked if I'd like to go out froggin'. Well, I was in the mood. What really hooked me, though, wasn't the frogs or the frog fries we used to have but seein' blue flames comin' from the exhaust of that airboat engine.

"I made up my mind to get me one. Soon after, I swapped my motorcycle for a sixty-five-horsepower airboat. We used to put our boats in at Andytown near where Alligator Alley (Route 84) inter-sects Route 27. It was just a gas station and a saloon owned by a man named Andy. We all used to meet there after work.

"You took your own tools with you on airboats. If a valve blew, you fixed it yourself or drifted till someone spotted you and hauled you out. It's easy to get in trouble in the Everglades. You can run out of fuel and get stranded. Or just get lost. I've helped plenty of people out of there.

"Before Route 27 became a major road, we used to jump our air-boats over it, sparks flying. We'd go over to Big Cypress Swamp in Indian territory.

"It was great. Some of the boys in those days used to get drunk, four sheets to the wind, you know, and drag-race their boats down Route 27. We burned out more than a few hulls. It was wild.

"I used to have me some swamp buggies back then too. They look like tanks and have treads. You can go through the swamps pretty well with them.

"I named my first one *Monster Mash*. I took two rebuilt engines from some old Cadillacs and rigged 'em inside. I also had a smaller buggy called *Midget Squish*. It went fifteen miles an hour and we used it to go out hunting for wild boars.

"I got interested in speed and gradually moved into airboats. My latest has a two-hundred-sixty-horsepower aircraft engine. I can go faster than fifty miles an hour. It just draws a few inches of water; it has to in the shallow Glades. I use it to get out to my camp eight miles from the Sawgrass recreation area.

"I got my camp from an old gator poacher who I'll just call Dan. He had a tiny two-room shack out there. If you weren't looking where you were going, you'd step outside and fall into water. We used it as a hunting lodge. In them days, there were plenty of ducks, bass, deer, wild hogs—everything.

"Dan was some kind of guy. In the thirties he'd go out for months in the Miami Canal in an old pushboat he poled up the sloughs. The Glades were too shallow to use a motor in, although he did try to use an old Model-A engine once. Said he worked on it more than he rode on it. He'd sleep on mudbanks over a tarp and stay out till he could get enough gators. That was before the hunting lodge.

"Dan taught me a lot about the Glades. What kinds of vegetation you can take an airboat through and what to steer clear of. He showed me the landmarks so I could pick my way out again. I learned where the main sloughs were, running north and south into Loxahatchee.

"Dan saved my life once. I got bit by a cottonmouth snake. He got me into the hospital. I swelled up some but, after six days, was ready to go back out into them Glades.

"Dan got some age on him and didn't want to mess with the camp no more. He said I could have it if I fixed it up. So every chance I got, I'd go out there with a shovel and wheelbarrow to haul mud. Built up a nice head of land and started from scratch, tearing down rooms and driving in pilings. I hauled in everything: lumber, fixtures, piping. I carpeted the downstairs and added a second story after a few floods. My home has all the creature comforts now.

"Because I know about electricity from working at FPL, I built my own electric generator out back. I have two modern bathrooms with flush toilets and I installed a septic system. I have me a color TV and use electric can openers and coffee grinders. You name it.

"Outside I put in two sodium streetlamps. You can see them lamps for miles out in the Glades. Only things like it around, since my closest neighbors are ten miles away in Camp Alley. After twenty years of sweat, I've shoveled out more than two hundred feet of land and lined it with cypress trees after the rabbits ate the first saplings I planted.

"It's beautiful in the Glades. I love it at night. Sometimes the moonlight sparkles on the sawgrass and everything just glitters. We get some hellish thunderstorms out here too. Sharp lightning storms that churn up all the water. I love the sound of rain pattering on the roof and I love fishing in the rain. I like waking up here and seeing the footprints of deer in the mud. And watchin' water snakes, coons, possums. And seein' the gators sunnin' themselves on the banks.

"For a while, I had some turtles here layin' eggs on the island. I discovered a hawk was stealing them away so I'd pick up the baby turtles and put them out of harm's way. Once I smelled skunk, but I know they hate water. That's a mystery—smelling skunks out here.

"I also used to have an owl's nest on the island. At night the mother owl would hide the eggs, and always in a different place. And there's millions of frogs. They'll be makin' lots of noise when, all of a sudden, they'll all go quiet at once. It's incredible. All this adds to the wonder and mystery of the Everglades."

—Interview by William Pohl

CARRABELLE

Riley Akers
John Summerhill

A SILVER-BLUE WATER TOWER proclaims to the world of pines, white clapboard houses, and Gulf hammock below, in bold, handpainted letters: "CARRABELLE, FLORIDA!"

Next to the water tower, Carrabelle has a few other landmarks of distinction: the world's smallest police station, housed in a telephone booth on Main Street, and Riley's Bait and Tackle Shop.

Riley's is the southern counterpart to the New England general store *cum* bait shop that abounds near the docks of Down East and Gloucester fishing villages. Like the New England stores, this one has an old-fashioned, homey feeling that places it more in a bygone era than in today's shopping mall generation.

Riley's cants out over wooden docks that give rise to a small, aging fleet of shrimpers and oyster dredges. The store is chock-a-block with useful items: Billy Beer, J. R. Ewing's Private Stock, fishing tackle, canned Campbell's pea soup, hunting knives, old-fashioned glass bottles of Coca Cola, an ancient serrated shark tooth, a six-foot-long rattlesnake skin, and numerous nautical miscellania, necessaries, and whatchamacallits.

Lining the shelved walls are wooden chairs and rockers, well-worn

Photo by Walter Michot

and broken in, each facing a small wood-burning stove. It's cold in the early winter morning in Carrabelle. Riley Akers, who owned the shop until his death in 1988, would hold forth with John Summerhill, his fishing buddy, and others like Captain Bruce Moore who chanced to wander in to gam away the time. Like frogs lined up on a log, the men would sit in a short row, their pregnant silences interspersed with yarns of Prohibition days, fish lies, and reminiscences about the good life in local fishing camps.

AKERS (tilting his chair back against the wall): "I'm from Tennessee but come down to Florida to fish fulltime back in 1950.

"My wife and I bought a forty-six-acre fishing camp on Three Rivers not far from Tate's Hell Swamp over by Yent's Bayou. Had furnished cottages on it. That was some swell place.

"When I first come into that camp it had some bad parties there. Pretty rough. A lot of guys down from Georgia out to have themselves a time. So I went over to see the sheriff in Apalachicola. I told him, 'Sheriff,' I says, 'Sheriff, I don't know what I got into but I aim to clean it up.'

"He says, 'Well, if you want, I'll deputize you. You just go ahead and clean it up. If you need help, holler for me.' I says I wasn't gonna need no help. I got me a gun and it didn't take long before the camp was clean.

"We used to house a hundred people in the cabins. You could go from the camp by boat up the Carrabelle River or you could fish in the saltwater bay. Caught trout, redfish, and largemouth bass. I had me about twelve guides including John Carr, Captain Chipman, Andy Delaney, Beaufort Duval, John Brown, Slim Evans, and yours truly. Most of them guys was characters.

"Slim Evans, for example, was a bootlegger and gator poacher. I once had a warden fishin' with me who run a federal penitentiary outside Atlanta. He recognized Slim when we met him upriver and asked, 'Ain't that Slim Evans?'

" 'Maybe it is and maybe it isn't,' I says.

" 'Well, he was a customer of mine a couple of times.'

"Slim used to catch gators with a line from his boat and kill them with a hatchet. Right between the eyes. Once he told me how a gator without a tail got up on its hind legs and chased him around. It would've caught old Slim if it hadn't got tangled in a tree. He tied its head off and shot it.

"Slim had arthritis real bad and was all gnarled up. He and Captain Chipman had them a little old black whiskey still up in the New River in Prohibition times. After they come in from guiding and cleaned out the fish, you could hear their boat motor heading back up the river. There was unmarked whiskey bottles left lying around the cabins. I later found the still up a path at the end of the creek. I says, 'You boys is going to get caught.'

" 'Oh, we ain't makin' no whiskey.'

"Well, two weeks later Chipman comes runnin' in scraped up and tells me how they caught old Slim. They took Slim before the judge, who knew him from four previous meetings. Slim shows the judge his knotted hands and says, 'You see, judge, I can't make no livin' like the next man. You can turn me loose and I'll try to make my way or you can put me up somewhere, feed me, and take care of me.'

"Well, that judge let him go. He figgered it was some cheaper to turn Slim loose than put him up in jail.

"Everyone was bootleggin' in them days. In Tennessee, them hill-billies was into it between coal mining. They all wore badges to keep from sellin' it to themselves.

"Andy Delaney was another character. Whoa! He owned the Delaney fish camp on the bay and always made a living. If there was nothing doing at the camp, he'd pick up scrap iron to sell. Got his start in life runnin' booze up the river. He had an old boat that burned naptha. The hotter it burned, the faster it went.

"Delaney was once runnin' moonshine when the law caught on and started chasin'. Each time he rounded a river bend, he'd dump off some jugs of stuff. Then he threw the boat in reverse and stopped, tethered it to a tree, poured some whiskey on hisself, and played possum.

"The law stopped when they saw Delaney. They hollered, shoved him with a foot, and decided to keep chasin' 'cause Delaney was too danged drunk to be the man they thought they was on to.

"Last time I saw Delaney he still knew where them jugs was he dumped overboard. But the corks had rotted out so the stuff was no good.

"Captain Chipman was an old-time deep sea fisherman who couldn't read or write but who knew more about the sea in the days when they was runnin' them old sailboats. He could get around with an old one-lunger scrappy engine no one else could manage. He sailed by the stars with a compass and knew what he was doing."

SUMMERHILL: "He sure did. You take these days with all them electronics. Today's fishermen would be lost without them. Like today, my children can't add without mashing a button on some computer. Same with navigation.

"Today's shrimpers use automatic pilots and sounding machines and radar. Few could punch their way out of a paperbag without machines. They even have scopes that show the schools of fish and bottom contours from an electronic map of the Gulf floor. The result? The whole place is overfished. The fish can't hide no more."

AKERS: "There used to be fourteen charter fishing boats out here. I shared two fifty-footers myself when I first came. We took seventy-two people out fishing for grouper and snapper. Now there's just two boats left. I opened this shop in 1962 as a ticket office. Stuffed in some bait and tackle, and in the mornings it used to take three people to wait on all the customers. Now you can spend all day setting around telling fish lies. It's quiet.

"When I first come here in 1950 snapper was eighteen cents a pound. Grouper fetched eight cents a pound. Today snapper is two dollars and ten cents a pound and grouper sells for one sixty-five if you can find it. Back then if you didn't bring in eight hundred pounds of fish a day with forty people you was foolin' around. Now if you catch eight hundred pounds in three days you're doing pretty fine.

"Pollution from the Saint Joe Paper Company don't help none either. When I first come here the shallows of the bay looked like a hay field with lots of seagrasses. Trout hid among the stalks. Today, because of pollution and the shrimpers that drag the bottom, the sea floor's as clean as the floor of this room. All the coral's been broke off.

"Apalachicola Bay is still knowed for its oysters and men still tong for them. You see guys with arms like gorillas and you know what they do for a living. But even them oysters is getting overfished."

SUMMERHILL: "You know a lot of things happen out on the ocean you can't explain. Like the time you saw a boat in the clouds, Riley."

AKERS: "Oh yeah. We saw a boat in the clouds one night. It was like light shining out from under the water. Erle Johnson saw a monster one night. He was on a commercial fishing boat and this head attached to a long neck come up out of the water and looked down on him. Swore he'd never go back out. And this man don't drink. Once I needed a licensed captain and offered Erle fifty dollars just to be on board. He still wouldn't go out.

"I saw something over yonder on John's boat the other day that looked like a piece of plywood on the water. We run over and I run up front and here was this fin. Forty feet behind it was the tail flipper! I said, 'My God, John, it's all in one piece.' Turned out to be a whale shark."

SUMMERHILL: "They're docile. They run with their mouth open and suck in plankton. Their mouth is as wide as a dinner table. We also see dolphins and blackfish that can run up to six hundred pounds. They'll follow you. We shoot in the air to scare them off, 'cause if they're with you, you don't catch another thing that day."

AKERS: "I used to watch this huge stingray off the west end of Dog Island. It was nine feet across and some guy from Tallahassee killed it. I was sad to see it go. But most of the time we just see normal junk.

"I remember getting caught once in a hundred-mile-an-hour squall. It came out of nowhere four years ago. We just let it blow and rode it out. It skinned the paint off the boat right down to the wood. The rigging was screaming like a steam whistle and the sea was all white foam."

SUMMERHILL: "Usually it's quiet in Carrabelle. Till the shrimpers come in, that is. They go out up to thirty days and when they get back, they all pile into the Edgewater Bar to drink and fight. The local cops call in the deputies from Apalachicola to haul these guys off. Once, Deputy Marvin shook down two guys who were slugging it out in the parking lot. When he was certain they had no guns or knives, he let them continue. It was one hell of a fight for fifteen minutes. Then they all went back in and drank more beer together. That's how it is."

AKERS (lowering voice and dropping chair back down on four legs):

"It used to be bootleggers. Now it's drugs. Most of the stuff is home-grown on Saint Joe Paper Company land or in the National Forest. You can tell when they harvest it. Suddenly everybody has new clothes and new pickups. All them drug people drive pickup trucks. What do you drive, John?"

SUMMERHILL: "A pickup. But that's not fair, Riley."

AKERS: "What do you drive, Captain Moore?"

MOORE: "A pickup. Why, Riley, what do you drive?"

AKERS (tilting chair back and smiling): "Just a regular car. I ain't in the business."

—Interview by William Pohl

John and Myrtle Irsak

IN 1885, HENRY FLAGLER BUILT St. Augustine's Ponce de Leon Hotel, ushering in a brief period of high-class tourism in the area; however, as Flagler pushed his railroad down the coast, he created access to a more tropical Florida, one which quickly captured the imaginations of winter visitors. For many years, the beaches near St. Augustine were bypassed and remained largely as they had always been. Only in recent times have population pressures changed that situation. Today, the drive along A1A between St. Augustine and Ormond Beach is largely a parade of huge condominiums, streamlined motels, and impressive seaside homes, but about a mile north of Matanzas Inlet is the Silver Sands Motel, a four-unit operation run by John and Myrtle Irsak.

The Silver Sands is a reminder of a time when accommodations for Florida's tourists were not so completely in the hands of international corporations offering hundreds of identical rooms. The Irsaks arrived in Summer Haven before the beaches of North Florida were discovered by large-scale developers, and they have watched with amazement as the coastline above and below them has turned from a secluded refuge to a teeming tourist area. In their years by the

Photo by Walter Michot

Atlantic, they have also seen the children of some of their steady customers grow to adulthood and start bringing their own offspring to the Silver Sands. The Irsaks' motel is the area's only remaining example of the type of cozy, family-run beach facility so familiar to an earlier generation of Florida vacationers.

The story of how they bought their land and built the Silver Sands with their own labor has the flavor of American pioneering. It certainly harks back to a time not so long ago, when beachfront property was still within the reach of average working people. The Irsaks have seen the value of their holdings grow to fabulous proportions by comparison with the modest investment that started their business, yet they politely refuse buy-out offers and continue as they have for twenty-nine years, attentively looking after the Silver Sands and the people who stay there.

JOHN IRSAK: "I'm hard of hearing, so I talk loud, but I don't hear loud. Why did I come here? I worked most of my life for the *Cleveland Plain Dealer*. There was a lotta newspapers in Cleveland. There was *The News Leader*. *News Leader* moved over to *The News* . . ."

MYRTLE IRSAK: "He wants to hear about Florida. We used to come down to Florida on vacation . . ."

MR. IRSAK: "When you're young, you look forward to the time you're gonna retire. Right? So, where am I gonna retire? In Cleveland, there's snow, although there was a lot of work. We had friends that were across the street from us, and then they sold their house and moved to Daytona. So we used to visit 'em. We used to go down A1A and one time we saw a sign on this property, 'For Sale.' We wound up paying five-and-a-half thousand dollars cash for this lot."

MRS. IRSAK: "When we came here, there was no houses from here on down to just before Marineland. There was nothing north, except one house up on the hill, and then quite a ways on there were four more that belonged to people that lived in Leesburg. And that's all there was here. You could go for hours and you wouldn't see a car."

MR. IRSAK: "Now it's one right after another. In the morning it's . . ."

MRS. IRSAK: "And they drive sixty, sixty-five, seventy miles an hour! You go out here to the mailbox and they almost knock you off of the road!"

MR. IRSAK: "You couldn't walk across this lot to the beach because this was all jungle here. We had to go down to the road and drive around to see what the beach looked like. The beach had thousands of shells. Women and men used to go down there and fill up bags of shells. All kinds. I don't know the names of all those shells. There's a name for every one of 'em, but I don't know 'em. Once in a while, you'll find one nowadays, but not very often. Everybody who goes down there picks up a shell, and there's a lot of people. On Saturday and Sunday it's Grand Central Station out there."

MRS. IRSAK: "The sand dollars. Remember those? We used to get scads of sand dollars. We used to keep a big tub full of shells up by the garage there, and then we'd let the people who came here take 'em home with 'em. We started doing that with friends from Ohio, who came down and helped us build the place. We bought the property in 1953, but we didn't start to build until 1960."

MR. IRSAK: "I could take ninety days off from the newspaper without losing my priority, so in the winter of '60, I come down pulling a ton of tools. We got to the Pennsylvania Turnpike and a guy says, 'You can't get on the Pennsylvania Turnpike because you don't have any brakes on your trailer.' So, we went on an alternate route through the Pennsylvania mountains and I can tell you that was a scary ride. On both sides there was those big semi's laying in the holes, it was so icy. We were lucky. I had an Oldsmobile with snow tires on it, and I'd have to go down the hill fast enough to be able to go up the next hill, but if I went too fast I would wind up in the brink like those big semi's."

MRS. IRSAK: "When we started building, we stayed down in the old Pelican Motel, the other side of Marineland. Ted and Ann Novak used to run that, but they both died. There's nothing in there now."

MR. IRSAK: "We did all the work ourselves. We had the foundation poured by somebody else, and had some of the rough plumbing and the plastering done, but everything else we did. I drew up the plans myself. They had to be signed by an engineer or a registered architect. Well, I wasn't a registered architect, so I paid an engineer twenty-five dollars to make corrections and sign 'em. He didn't make a single change."

MRS. IRSAK: "We were told, 'If you put kitchenettes in those rooms, why you'll never rent 'em. People come to the beach to get away from that.' Now, that's all I can rent, is my kitchenettes! Right from the beginning I'd have people who'd come here and stay all winter. I have one from Indiana, and I have Canadians that are here now, that come every year, because I have three kitchenettes. This fellow in here, he's from Ohio. That white car's his. He has been coming for I don't know how many years. And he comes the first of September and goes home probably the first of May or June. You wouldn't believe it, but this place is recommended all over the eastern United States. One person tells another, you know."

MR. IRSAK: "Place looks like a junkyard, but they like it. People who stay here generally come back."

MRS. IRSAK: "This place is more like a home than it is a motel. I had an old man who was here, you know, and he says, 'Mrs. Irsak, I wanna know what you do to your sheets. When I get in bed at night, they smell so good!' And I said, 'Oh, I hang 'em out there in that sun and salt.' And he just died laughing. I've always done that with my sheets. The type of people we get in here are real easy to work with, and so many of 'em stay so long. Like this woman from Indiana. I only change the beds every two weeks. And she will take off the sheets and bring 'em to me and say, 'Myrtle, gimme the sheets and I'll make the beds. I got 'em changed already.' So all I gotta do is wash the sheets. And she's clean as a pin! When she leaves, the room looks like when she moved in."

MR. IRSAK: "You can park your car right in front of your room. It's more convenient."

MRS. IRSAK: "Four units is just right. I couldn't take no dozen cars sittin' out there. This way it don't bother me at all. But a dozen cars out there, I'd go crazy. I'd leave. One reason people love it here is 'cause it's quiet. We built back from the ocean behind the dunes 'cause I didn't want that wind hitting me all the time. And I wanted far enough off of the street so you could sleep and didn't have cars making racket all night long. See, we have walls out there eight inches thick. Johnny put up the blocks and this friend of mine, her and I, we filled those holes in those blocks with that insulation . . ."

MR. IRSAK: "Vermiculite."

MRS. IRSAK: "Yeah, and you don't hear nothing. I had a couple here from Vermont, I think they were, and they tape-recorded the waves down on the beach and then they brought it in the room and listened to it at night when they went to bed. So she wrote me a card, and she said, 'Boy am I glad we made that tape! We go to sleep every night with that tape going.' And that German couple out there right now, they sleep all day, but they bum around at night, I guess. I never know when they come in. And then they sleep. The other day she said, 'You know, we were tired and lazy. We slept till twelve o'clock.' In daytime! Now anyplace else, you couldn't do that because there's too much noise. We stayed in a motel one night and we didn't sleep a wink because the couple in the next room were fightin'. Oh, you never heard such fightin' in all your life! We don't get that kinda people. Those kinda people, they don't wanna be where there's small bunches, see? They wanna be where gangs are, so they can really carry on. Even the man who owns that place on the lot next door says, 'You got a good bunch that comes over there. You never have any trouble.' Anyway, you'd be surprised at the people that say, 'Boy, I don't know, but you sure got good insulation in these rooms.' I say, 'Yep. I know it. We put it there.'"

MR. IRSAK: "We've got an eight-inch wall there, with the vermiculite down inside, you see."

MRS. IRSAK: "He knows that. We put quite a bit of planning into the place. Now, Johnny wanted to put the entrances on the other side, but I said, 'No. I don't want that. I want to be on this side, so we're facing the south. This way, we'll get the sun in the wintertime.' It comes right up to the windowsills on the porch there. In the summertime, you got no sun there at all. You can sit there all day if you want to! You'd be surprised that we can sit right out here on our porch on the coldest winter days, and you don't even need a sweater or anything. All that wind goes up and goes over you because we're in behind the dunes."

MR. IRSAK: "You don't get the salt from the ocean. Those people that are right on the ocean have to come out and wash their windows every day."

MRS. IRSAK: "I wouldn't want to live up there for nothin'. We've never even had any damage from hurricanes."

MR. IRSAK: "Hurricane Donna smashed your car in '64! Tell about that."

MRS. IRSAK: "Donna didn't do it."

MR. IRSAK: "Who done it then?"

MRS. IRSAK: "It was my own fault 'cause I parked it in the wrong place. That happened when I was down here running the place by myself. I ran it for the first seven years. He didn't come, except for three months in the winter when he got off work. Anyway, one of our friends called up before Donna hit and she says, 'Come and stay with me. Bring the cat.' They lived facing the ocean. So, the wind blew in their big glass door and blew this big post over. It must have been six by six. Landed right down the top of my car. I said, 'I'da been better off if I'd stayed home!' And I come home and I didn't have nothing wrong! And the winds was a hundred and fifty miles an hour! That's why I say the next time we have a good hurricane, it's gonna go right in the doors of all these condominiums! If they would-a built them farther back it might-a been all right, but, you see, they're all right on that ocean. I've seen it happen before. You know where the big motel is, down by the pier in St. Augustine Beach? There was a fellow there that had cottages; he had a half a dozen of 'em, I guess. And he had a restaurant and there was a skating rink there, too. Well, we was having one of those storms out in the Atlantic that was making the waves come up. That was when I was here by myself, and I had a friend staying with me from up north. Well, we went down and watched the water come in and go right under those cottages. All that went right in the ocean, the cottages and everything."

MR. IRSAK: "The Tradewinds had a restaurant on top of the hill, and that was washed out, and it collapsed in the water."

MRS. IRSAK: "That's what I'm saying."

MR. IRSAK: "Oh."

MRS. IRSAK: "I've seen those dunes go. You got two of 'em up there and then all of a sudden, you've got one, or a half of one! If it'd been me, I would-a said, 'No condominiums along here, period.'"

MR. IRSAK: "But nowadays you couldn't do what we did. Too expensive. See, we can make out 'cause I own this place lock, stock, and barrel."

MRS. IRSAK: "We don't owe a dime to nobody."

MR. IRSAK: "But somebody else couldn't buy it and do what we do, 'cause there's not enough income to carry a big mortgage."

MRS. IRSAK: "A real estate woman told us some guy from Georgia wanted to buy our place. He had stayed here one time and he liked it so well he wanted to give us four hundred thousand for it. But I said, 'This is my home. I'm happy here. I don't have a lotta neighbors next door to fight with like they have other places. I get nice people here. I enjoy talkin' with 'em, visitin' with 'em.' Yep. I feel just as good as I did when I was fifty or before, and I'm gonna be eighty years old the last day of March. Never been sick a day in my life, not even a headache. I tell people that, and they don't believe it. When I was born my mother was in bed with chicken pox. So the doctor says, 'Well, it'll either kill the baby or make her immune to all diseases.' All diseases, he said. And it did! Everybody wants to know, 'When you gonna start showing your age?' and I say, 'When the good Lord wants me to, I guess.' I always ate right and I lived right. I never drank, smoked, or any of that stuff. There was a guy here one day, sittin' out on the front porch drinkin' beer, you know. I was talkin' to him, and he says, 'Could I get you a can of beer?' I said, 'No thank you, sir! This is my castle and I'm very particular what goes into it.' He liked to died a-laughin'. I'm gonna live to be a hundred. Even Johnny—we've been married fifty-eight years, and he's never been sick either. We're gonna be right here for some time to come."

MR. IRSAK: "At age eighty-four, where you gonna go?"

—Interview by John Ames

Photo by Walter Michot

Fred Knoller

FRED KNOLLER IS THE "Grand Master" of bicycle racing. His spindly legs sprout from baggy shorts, his shoulders are rounded, his voice cracks. The nonagenarian has ridden so many miles, his hip bones have worn out and have been replaced with plastic joints several times. And still he rides, working out along Route A1A on his silver bicycle to keep in shape. In 1981, at the age of eighty-five, he placed among the top contenders in a forty-seven-kilometer race through the Tyrolean Alps. In the following interview, conducted in 1985, he recounts a lifetime of racing back to World War I, when he competed at the Velodrome in New Jersey.

"I WAS BORN A LEO in East Orange, New Jersey, in 1896. I lived there and in Milburn, a suburb of Newark that rests along the Lakawanna Railroad. I dropped out of high school to work in my father's bakery and later as a cookie salesman. We had two Model-A Fords which we used to deliver bread. I drove.

"I didn't get bicycle-riding fever until 1912. I was about sixteen years old. Working in the bakery was good 'cause I could get off any-

Photo by Henry Rowland

time I wanted to work out at the Valesburgh Velodrome, where they held the bike races each Wednesday and Sunday. Those races drew larger crowds than baseball games, including the ones in Yankee Stadium.

"We also used to go to Jersey City, Montreal, and the Newark baseball grounds to watch bicycle races. In summer, the open-air trolleys were full of people, some standing on the running boards, all going to see the races. Nickel a ride. Bells ringing. The motorman and money collector loved race days. They made a lot of money.

"I remember the first time I saw the bike races. I was about fifteen. A neighbor took me to the old Madison Square Garden in New York to watch a six-day race. Part of it anyway. That was a hundred and forty-four hours of bike racing. Two riders were on each team. While one was riding, the other relaxed or slept on a bunk by the side of the track. Everyone followed the results in the *Newark News*. The standings of the riders were published on the front page each day. It was exciting.

"I had a trainer at the time, Fred Kitts. He was a butcher and trained us in his spare time. We'd take the Maplewood trolley to the Velodrome or I'd ride my road bike eight miles to the track, hang it in the rafters, and take down my racing bike.

"Kitts would start me, time me, and grab the bike when I dismounted, 'cause in those days there were no brakes. The bike had one fixed gear and riders had to be powerful to get up their wind and speed. We wore golfer's gloves with no fingers. They had leather padding on the palms. We used the gloves to reach down on the wheel rims to slow the bikes. During races we didn't wear the gloves. We'd backpedal and stop by dragging our legs. Kitts gave us rubdowns after we were through.

"I had a robe in those days that I'd wear after I got back sweaty. I also used that robe to cover the tires to keep them out of the sun. They were thin tires, made of rubber latex, and they had one hundred twenty-five pounds of air pressure in them. In the sun they'd pop if they got hot enough. They sounded like revolvers when they burst.

"I started training in 1915 at the Velodrome. In 1916 I entered my first race. Everyone started together in the amateur races. The better riders broke into the lead. They could ride one-eighth of a mile in

11.2 seconds. That's forty-five miles an hour on a one-speed bike. They were powerful riders.

"Prizes were certificates up to twenty dollars from sporting goods stores like Bamberger's or Holt Jewelers.

"When I was seventeen I came in second in a race and got my first novice medal. I saw an opportunity to enter that race at the Velodrome. I only had my road bike with heavy tires, no headlamp, and my pump, giving it extra weight. Still I got out and stayed in front behind one fellow. The railbirds in the bleachers cheered me on. Only later did I learn I came in just behind Fred Taylor, the champ.

"After World War One, I went to race in Philadelphia against the Harris Brothers, Frank and George. They were black. Best in the sport. They won all the races. There were about thirty competitors. I sat at the rear wheels of Frank Harris to pace myself and see if I could keep up. I got second place. The other brother came in third. That was a red-letter day for me.

"In 1919 there was the Mayor Gillen Stakes in Newark. It was run on a half-mile dirt track, packed down by horses. Again I entered with my road bike. It took me a lap to catch the limit men. I caught up to an old warhorse named Buck who pulled me the rest of the way. I stayed by him and in the bell lap—the last lap of the race—I passed Tony Young. I had a good sleigh ride with Young on my tail. I had to fight him off at the turns and down the stretch. He was six feet four inches tall and had long legs and longer elbows. He used them both. The judges didn't see nothing.

"I thought this Tony Young would get me in the last hundred yards so I dug in as best I could along the railing. Well, I beat him! I knew I'd place in the money but never thought I'd win. Surprised the hell out of myself. I was so refreshed when all my friends came out yelling, 'Fred, you did it! You upset the applecart.' When they told me who I beat, I was amazed. Young later went on to the Olympics. Thinking back on it, *I* could have gone on to the Olympics.

"In those days we also used to run pursuit races like one around the baseball field in Berwick, Pennsylvania. That was in 1918. You're started at intervals and ride until you catch the man in front of you. The race goes on until there are only two contenders.

"It took nine miles of racing before someone finally caught up with me. I rode forty-five laps that race. To keep going was a question of psychology. You had to keep your mind going. If you thought to yourself, 'I'm not going to make it,' you'd lose. If you thought, 'The other guy's just as tired as me,' and ride faster, you'd win. The old vaudeville saying, 'It ain't what you used to have but what you got now that counts,' still enters my mind. Even now in my eighties.

"I keep trying. I'm the oldest active bicycle racer in the world. The second oldest is Ed Delano, 'Foxy Grandpa.' He's nine years younger than I. We go back together a long time. He showed me a caricature once in 'Ripley's Believe It or Not.' It was supposed to be me. I'm also listed in the *Guinness Book of World Records*.

"I try to keep in shape. I logged more than seventy-five miles a week on bikes, well into my eighties. Now I walk two miles a day on the beach. My calisthenics normally include ten chinups, forty push-ups, and fifteen situps. Right now after my last operation I'm down to about four chinups and weigh a hundred and twenty pounds.

"I started to have hip troubles around 1949. My hips gave way from the cycling and aggravated rheumatism. When X-rays were taken they discovered osteoarthritis. The right hip was shot. I was taking aspirin before cycling twenty-five miles each morning. I had to get the hip replaced. The new one works great. It's plastic with a stainless steel joint. A little arch goes down into my thigh bone. The hip socket is made of acrylic. I replaced the left hip too, and when the right one wore out again, I replaced it a second time. That was in 1984.

"Up until this last operation I used to go to the Nationals, as I have since they started in 1976. I raced before 1976 against youngsters forty years and up. There was no one else in my league. Now they have a race for veterans like me.

"I won the Nationals in my division in 1982. I was eighty-six. I raced twenty-five miles out of Boulder, Colorado, and finished in one hour and twenty-seven minutes. I took a victory lap around the mall when I got in. My fans were waiting for me.

"At the end of that race my pulse was one-twenty-four. Some twenty-year-olds finish a race like that and are up around one-seventy-four. I was in the peak of physical conditioning.

"I never raced professionally. Just did it for exercise and pleasure. My girlfriend says I should be able to continue. She wants to see me at the Nationals when I'm ninety years young. I aim to be there."

—*Interview by William Pohl*

Don Grooms

DON GROOMS HAS BEEN WRITING, singing, and teaching about American Indians and American folk history for more than twenty-five years.

He was midwifed by an old Cherokee "granny woman" in a shack on an isolated mountaintop in what is now the Great Smoky Mountains National Park in North Carolina. He says he's a "full-fledged mongrel—part Cherokee, part Creek, and part Irish."

Although Grooms's closest friends are Cherokee Indians, he became guitar-picking buddies with a young Seminole warrior, James Billie. When Billie became chief of the Seminoles, Grooms became a consultant for the tribe and a spokesman for their causes.

Grooms has been playing music since the age of three, when he practiced on a cigar box banjo. By age six he had moved on to a guitar, and by age fourteen he was playing for a bluegrass band and had made his first record. His Indian protest songs range from "blatant humor to blatant exploitation of the white man's guilt," and include "Chief Vitachuco" (summarizing four hundred years of Florida Indian history) and "Congratulations, Standing Bear" (recounting the 1879 court case when the U.S. courts first ruled that an Indian is a human being).

Today, Grooms teaches journalism at the University of Florida, is author of a "worst-selling" book called *How To Talk Trash In Cherokee*, and remains in demand at folk music festivals. Growing up neither Cherokee nor white, he is a dispassionate observer of both, and values their oral traditions.

"I WAS BORN ON the coldest night in the coldest month in the coldest state in the South. That was January 12, 1930, in North Carolina. Haven't been warm since.

"I'm one-fourth Cherokee, one-fourth Irish, one-fourth Scotch and one-fourth Old Milwaukee.

"Florida is an interesting state. All the Yankees congregate on the seacoasts. You get two miles away from the coast and you're back in deep Cracker country. Alligator hunters. Cattle ranchers. Seminoles.

"Florida, like the rest of the country, is getting raped. I write songs to try to get the rest of the world to pay attention. It's like I'm fighting the introduction of barbed wire. When it was introduced to America, all these guys who had wandered freely across America suddenly couldn't anymore. Up in the hills of North Carolina, I wrote about the land developers who were cuttin' mountains up to create more homesites for Yankee tourists. My brother, twenty years ago, bought twenty acres for two hundred dollars. Now that same land's going for twenty thousand an acre. The people who live there can't afford to buy land anymore. When they look out on their mountains all they see are A-frames and vacation cottages and No Trespassing signs. I have one song called 'A-Frame-Covered Blue Ridge Mountain Blues.'

"I remember when Champion Paper and Fiber Company bought two whole mountains and put No Hunting, No Fishing, No Trespassing signs up. The people who lived there burned down those mountains. They said, 'If we can't use them, nobody can.'

"A man here in Gainesville had an old bicycle shop with thousands of used bikes and parts he kept in his front yard. Developers came in wanting his land for another shopping mall. When he refused to sell, they had him committed to a mental institution. Ran right over him. I hate things like that.

"Another developer came in here, a charcoal corporation. It put up a small plant and soon after sold out, leaving chemical debris all over the place. It killed the plants, the animals, the fish—everything that once lived here in harmony. I wrote a song about that.

"Florida is fast becoming one big Disney World. People come down here to make a fast buck. They have no concern for land or for the people and animals who live on the land. If there was a buck to be made, they'd sell their own mothers.

"There's lots of nonproductive things down here: drug smuggling, insurance. The University of Florida in Gainesville is a liberal oasis in a sea of conservatism. It attracts not only students but drifters and opportunists. There's also the rednecks. Country people: hunters, fishermen, mechanics, farmers, loggers, rock pit laborers. They can be territorial. During hunting season, it's 'This is *my* hog country.' If some stranger comes in to hunt 'their' hogs, that stranger might not wander out again.

"Now this place is becoming condo city. It's becoming hard for people like me to live here. There's less and less room for country people. The developers take over and the land becomes private. If the state takes over land to make a park, rules are posted and the place becomes inaccessible. Sometimes after five o'clock at night. Sometimes forever.

"You used to be able to innertube down the entire Ichetucknee River any time. It was so clear you could see the beer cans on the bottom. Now it's restricted. Every time barbed wire goes up, it means there's a steadily diminishing area where the human beings can live.

"I love to talk about the Seminoles. The word *Seminole* is a Spanish corruption of *Cimarron* which the Conquistadors took to mean 'outlaws' or 'runaways' who escaped when the rest of the natives were taken prisoner or killed. The Seminoles are actually a collection of native Indian nations from Florida.

"Around 1775 there were some thirty thousand Indians in Florida. When the whites came in, they decided to systematically wipe them out. All of them. The Indians were considered animals which didn't have souls.

"There were about twenty thousand Timucuans in the early 1700s. They were wiped out by the whiteskin diseases, materialism and exploitation. Then the Muskogees moved in. They had lived around creek beds in Georgia, Alabama, South Carolina, and Florida. They were nicknamed the Creeks, and by the end of the nineteenth century, they too were down to about one hundred and fifty in number.

"There were also the Miccosukees. Today there are only about twenty-one hundred of them left. Some sixteen hundred live under the rule of Chief Jim Billie. Another six hundred live along the Tamiami Trail. At this moment, a subtribe of them under Chief Buffalo Tiger are very hostile, not only to whites but to other Seminoles which Tiger considers to be 'white-skinned Indians.'

"These Miccosukees stay back in the swamps; you in Indian country there. I wouldn't go in there—might not come out again. They're very protective of their way of life and figure that all contact with whites so far has been of no benefit to them.

"When the whites got through with the Indian wars, there were just a handful of Miccosukees, Timucuans, Yamasee, Calusas, and Muskogees surviving. It was the closest this country ever came to committing genocide.

"In the 1930s there were only some three hundred Seminoles left. They lived back in the swamps around Everglades City. Medicine man Josie Billie and Richard Osceola took care of them until someone went in and said, 'Okay, you can come out now.' A small plot of land was negotiated for the Indians to live on, but no papers were signed.

"In the 1950s, remnants of the remaining Indians got together and formed the Seminole Tribe and corporation. Today, every four years, they get together to elect a tribal chairman and a president to develop economic programs. They started out raising cattle. Land was leased to citrus growers. Today, Chief [James] Billie and his lawyers are trying to get back that land so the profits can return to the Seminoles.

"You know, technically, the Seminoles remain at war with the United States. The Seminoles never signed peace treaties to get federal funds.

"Seminoles used to fight with spears. Now they fight with lawyers. Jim Billie and I have been friends since 1971 and he has told me how, as tribal chairman, he's helped to develop economic programs for the tribe. He studied how the Catholic church operates. He saw how it had tax-free land and could legally host bingo games. He saw his own people, in the meantime, eating fish and mosquitoes.

"Well, Billie got him some lawyers, borrowed a million dollars, and set up this big hut on reservation land in Hollywood and later one in Big Cypress. He set up bingo parlors. For the dignity of his people, he hired low-class whites to work there.

"By Florida law, you could only play bingo for a jackpot three nights a week. Billie learned that state laws don't apply on an Indian reservation. Today, seven nights a week, busloads of whites come in with their money. In 1983, the tribe made from bingo games eight million dollars. In 1984, they made sixteen million dollars. Billie beat the white man at his own game.

"The bingo money is used to build senior citizen centers, civic centers, and recreation areas on the reservation. Each Seminole gets about six hundred dollars quarterly from bingo revenue.

"Jim Billie also served in the Vietnam War and watched how the government PX stations sold cigarettes tax-free. He told his lawyers about that too. Today on the Hollywood reservation off Route 84, Indians sell cigarettes tax-free.

"The state of Florida is contesting this because it's losing some fifteen million dollars each year in revenues. Billie points out that those who pay taxes get police protection, medical clinics, and public schools in return. Seminoles have their own reservation counterparts—even their own police.

"Reservation police are different. When some Seminole kids get stopped for speeding, the tribal police may just take their keys and drive them home with a reprimand. We don't need a courthouse. We can hold court under a tree. It was different in the days when Indians were tried in federal courts.

"Another thing the Seminoles started are these big ponds to farm catfish to sell to the whiteskins. Billie also got a hundred and eighty thousand dollars from the feds to train young Seminoles to assemble high-tech materials. They work with major organizations like NASA.

"Every Christmas, Jim Billie loves to take over the Diplomat Hotel in Hallandale for the annual Seminole party. It's quite a scene. Here are these doormen in top hats and frockcoats opening gilded doors for big fat Seminole women! It's a big change from the swamps.

"Of course, there's some intermarriage and assimilation with lots of tribes. The Seminole reservation in Hollywood is on the edge of northern Miami. Young Indians drive AMC sports cars and listen to stereos. There are efforts to preserve the native heritage but assimilation is a fact of life.

"Still, it's very pleasurable for me to remain among my own kind of people out on Big Cypress Reservation or down in the Thousand Islands off Everglades City. That's where the unassimilated Indians live as they have for hundreds of years."

—*Interview by William Pohl*

Photo by Henry Rowland

Gene Schuler

FLORIDA IS THE NATION'S most popular retirement state and boasts a variety of "adult" communities ranging from Century Village to Leisureville. Perhaps it is no surprise, then, that thrown in with former stockbrokers and ad execs are a few baboons and tigers.

Baboons? Tigers? Yes, and more, residing today at the Wild Animal Retirement Village, nestled on an old ranch amid the pine barrens of rural Waldo. This menagerie of abused and abandoned "exotic" animals have been rescued and taken in over the years by former Hoxie Brothers Circus trainer Gene Schuler and his wife, Rusti, at their own expense. The Schulers have the compassion and expertise to handle and care for everything from malnourished pet alligators to an old circus lion with a curved spine and cleft palate.

"These animals have come to know us, trust us, and love us," says Gene Schuler. "As Native American Chief Joseph once said, 'If you can't give us a place to live, then give us a place to die.' We do what we can to offer animals who have no place else to go in this world a life of dignity."

Photo by Henry Rowland

"I HAVE ALWAYS LOVED ANIMALS. As a boy growing up in rural Pennsylvania, the woods were close. I spent my time hunting crawfish, birds, and snakes. I recall being yelled at by my mother when she discovered we had sixty frogs in the cellar along with a few turtles, pigeons, and rabbits. Of course, the kinds of animals I handle now—lions, tigers, and alligators—weren't available.

"I came down to Miami in 1959 and worked for the Hoxie Brothers Circus, a traveling mud show. I was the stock boss and trainer. We all doubled up. The lion trainer might sell balloons after the act. I had to ensure the diet, feed, and health of our animals. I also trimmed horses' feet, ran a pony ride, worked to put up tents, and settled occasional beefs for Hoxie Tucker, the old man.

"I also worked with wild animals in zoos. I have claw scars on my legs and shoulders from the big cats. Over time, I've come to understand these animals better.

"This place here used to be called the Old Buffalo Ranch. It was a tourist attraction and had a goat that walked a high wire, longhorn steers, six-gun shootouts, a log cabin saloon, and a herd of buffalos. I first saw the place when I was with the circus. We had some surplus trick ponies. At the time, Man Mountain Jimmy Dean, the wrestler, was here. He agreed to take the ponies from us and I delivered them. I got interested in the place.

"When Interstate 75 was built it took traffic away from Route 301 here, and the Old Buffalo Ranch closed down. It was defunct for fifteen years.

"My wife, Rusti, and I were living in Ocala at the time. The place was zoned for agriculture. Lots of people had horses and dogs. We took our first big cat in there, a lion named Stanley who was born with a massive cleft palate. Everything he ate or drank came back up through his nose. The fellow that owned him knew nothing about animals and kept the lion in a cage with two Doberman Pinschers. He fed the lion dog food and it developed a severe calcium deficiency and curvature of the spine. One of his legs had to be put in a cast. His bones were so soft he couldn't stand up.

"Stanley was under a court order to be destroyed. Rusti and I got him that afternoon. When we went to the judge, she wouldn't release him. Said it was someone else's property. We had to go to the state attorney to get custody.

"We took Stanley home and I built a cage for him. Our neighbors started coming around with their kids. They began to think he was some sort of attraction, but we were just trying to help the animal. He was not a display and we didn't have time for visitors.

"We soon took in Sheba, a lioness. Her owner didn't conform to the caging and sanitation regulations of the state. She once busted her shoulder getting out of her cage. Now she has a steel plate in it.

"We had to leave Ocala when it started to get too congested. I fully understand someone living next door who may have young children and be scared to death. We left for more space and lived near Gainesville on thirty-five acres. In 1979 we came to the Old Buffalo Ranch. There's no one around here for miles to complain.

"We incorporated into the Wild Animal Retirement Village to provide these poor animals with an alternative to death. Some had been mistreated. Others were sick, crippled, old or somehow imperfect. All were unwanted. We seek to provide a temporary home for whatever we can release back into nature. We'll take in owls, snakes, opossums, alligators, baby deer, hawks, raccoons, and exotic animals. We're not, however, a dumping station for stray dogs or cats. That, unfortunately, is what the Humane Society is for. It's very sad they have to kill many animals. I couldn't kill an animal just because it wasn't wanted.

"One problem for animals is people. People who buy a young animal and don't know anything about it.

"Love isn't enough. To raise a wild animal you need qualified people. You must be willing to clean up after the animal. You must understand its diet and social needs. You have to worry about their safety. Love is just not enough.

"As the animal grows, it becomes more expensive to keep, the novelty wears off, and they can grow dangerous as they reach sexual maturity. That's when they're given away.

"I've grown cynical. Unwanted animals are sent to research labs or destroyed. Society has its values all screwed up. It worries about the latest cars, deodorant, and the National Football League. If the last tiger disappears tomorrow, it's felt it wouldn't affect people.

"Society is callous. Many of the people living in cities and suburbs in South Florida came from concrete jungles. They don't miss what they never had: trees, animals, nature. We're all so stupid. We cut down trees that give off oxygen. We kill 'pests' that are part of the food chains. We're out of balance and at war with nature. We can send a man to the moon but we still cannot take chemicals and make another tiger. The last tiger may be extinct someday. The next in line may be us.

"We live here in the middle of Rednecksville. For many, their animal vocabulary consists of 'critter' and 'varmint.' Their idea of a good time is to take the dogs out and run raccoons. Or open up a six-pack and let the dogs fight. They could care less if the last animal died tomorrow or if they were the ones to have shot it. That's what we're up against.

"We owe a lot to animals. Aspirin, castor oil, our medical products—testing depends on animals. We have an obligation to take in animals from research labs. That's part of what my place is about.

"We have almost a hundred animals here. Three baboons I took off a truck from an animal dealer who was coming from the Metro Zoo. There's a Bengal tiger. We have Spiderman, an alligator who was dying of starvation. Today he's back from twenty pounds to two-twenty-five.

"A day doesn't go by when we don't get a brochure from some animal organization asking for a donation. Until recently no one gave us a quarter and we're working hands-on. We're not as politically involved as some other organizations, fund-raising and paying for salaries, gas, newsletters, and lobbying. We're out here trying to save animals and to provide a tangible alternative. Our money goes to the animals themselves.

"We're not a roadside zoo. We ask no admission charge, just donations. Our incorporation gives us the right to solicit funds.

"You know, I'm not justifying this place. None of these animals belong in cages. I have mixed feelings, but we don't live in a perfect world. Sometimes I wonder if we're providing an ark or a prison. But then there's this feeling of obligation. There is no other alternative for these animals. Except death. Maybe this place will raise the conscience of people someday."

—Interview by William Pohl

Melvin Fisher

MELVIN FISHER SEARCHED THE WATERS off the Florida Keys for decades to find the $40,000 gold necklace he wears around his neck. He found it amid a trove of treasure, using seventeenth-century maps and twentieth-century electronic sensors.

Research, business acumen, and luck led Fisher to a tantalizing trail of artifacts buried in the silt—the remains of the Terra Firma fleet, hidden for more than 300 years. The galleons, laden with New World riches, were destined for Spain to finance King Philip's military and national debt. Most of the fleet foundered off the Keys in a hurricane in 1622, spilling the valuable contents as the ships tumbled to watery graves.

The lost ships became the stuff of legend and captivated Fisher. He incorporated Treasure Salvors, a Key West–based salvage company, and raised monies from scores of investors to fund a fleet of salvage vessels, flagshipped by the *Dauntless*. With his family and crew, he combed the barrier reefs, searching against the odds for the lost vessels.

In 1971, Fisher made history when he found the anchor that eventually led him to *Nuestra Señora de Atocha*, one of the treasure ships.

Photo by Walter Michot

Records of its manifest showed that it had contained 550 passengers, 1,038 silver ingots, 7,175 ounces of gold, 230,000 hand-stamped silver coins, and a wealth of emeralds and jewels. It took weeks just to haul up the yield, including King Philip's heavy cannons. In 1985, Fisher found more gold jewelry and bars of silver, this time with the discovery of the *Santa Margarita*, another Terra Firma vessel.

Today, hundreds of millions of dollars in artifacts is owned by Treasure Salvors' investors; after years of legal maneuvering the courts ruled that, under state and admiralty laws, the finders could remain keepers.

"I GREW UP IN Hobart, Indiana, raising chickens with my father before taking up scuba diving. That's quite a change of professions, I guess. I pioneered in skin diving and sold some of the first aqualungs from Mel's Aquashop, a store I built in California from lobsters. I dived for lobsters in those days and for every ton I sold, I'd build another wall of my shop. That was in 1948. Now there's more than six hundred such stores in Los Angeles alone.

"I also ran a scuba diving school with fifteen instructors. We taught some sixty-five thousand people to enjoy life underwater. I began to experiment with underwater photography and had a television show that encouraged hundreds to buy scuba gear.

"I started an amateur salvage club. We'd dive for gold in the rivers of California using some dredges I developed. We hunted for jade in coves. We found plenty of both. We also dove in the ocean on the old gambling wrecks once owned by gangsters like Al Capone in the twenties and thirties. In fact, I still have the roulette wheel from Capone's ship. That's how I got interested in shipwrecks.

"To locate shipwrecks I started going to public libraries. I sorted through a hundred years of news clips and created my own library of facts. I know where wrecks are located off the coast of California and what they might contain. I have also studied documentation at the Library of Congress and Lloyds of London, which insured many of these ships. The paperwork tells where the ships sank.

"In 1963 I sold my business and came to Fort Pierce, Florida, to treasure hunt. I found a few gold doubloons, dazzling on the ocean floor, worth more than a million dollars. I salvaged them from a Spanish galleon that sank in 1715. That kind of experience can have an effect on you. It was an incentive to keep looking. Gold shines forever, brilliant, blinding, passed from hand to hand, man to woman. I got gold fever. I've been treasure hunting ever since.

"I'm not interested in modern wrecks but in dredging colonial history from Spanish galleons, English man-o'-wars, slavers, and privateers that sunk three hundred years ago. Archaeology and culture grows on you. It's better than the money.

"Salvage work is nothing new. Key West used to have its 'wreckers.' For years they salvaged cargos. The admiralty court across the street from my museum in Key West would adjudicate who got to keep what. Bounty was auctioned off the courthouse steps. Of course, some of the wreckers were corrupt and moved channel markers. They caused the wrecks and then got to the scene first to collect the cargo. In my salvage work, I get to the scene of wrecks three hundred years later.

"To find shipwrecks, I use a fleet of vessels including the *Dauntless*. My ships range from forty feet to one-sixty-seven feet in length. We stay out as long as weather and supplies hold out. Lots of talents are involved. You have divers, accountants, lawyers, archaeologists, electronics engineers, and mechanics. It's complex.

"It takes a trained eye to locate a wreck. We use about fifteen kinds of detection devices to sort through silt, mud, coral and . . . history.

"Modern history of Florida began in 1513 with Ponce de Leon's search for a new passage to India and for the Fountain of Youth. For two hundred years the Spanish controlled this hemisphere. Spain laid claim to the Caribbean Islands, South and Central America, and Florida.

"Look at the 1622 Terra Firma fleet. Its twenty-eight Spanish galleons were sent over to help the king replenish his war-depleted treasury. The ships brought in manufactured goods from Europe—cloth, wine, ironwork, papal indulgences—and exchanged them at annual fairs in Cartagena, Portobello, and Vera Cruz for New World exports: gold, silver, copper, indigo, and tobacco. Much of the silver was mined by Indian slaves from Potosi Mountain in South America. More than three hundred million pesos in coins and bullion were taken out. They're still mining what has become a crater, five hundred years later. Treasure gathered from all over the world was organized in Havana, Cuba, to be shipped back to Spain. Consequently, there are rich hunting grounds off the Keys here.

"The Terra Firma fleet stocked up on New World treasures and set sail out of Havana well into hurricane season. On the way back a northeaster swept the ships into the Straits of Florida. Nine of the twenty-eight galleons were stranded or sunk, including the *Nuestra Señora de Atocha* and the *Santa Margarita*, on the sixth of September, 1622. We knew from more than forty-five thousand documents that those ships sank somewhere between the Florida Keys and the Dry Tortugas. Finding them was like looking for a needle in a haystack.

"When a ship sinks it doesn't go down all at once. A thirty-foot wave would pick up a galleon and smash it on a reef, dragging it two hundred feet. Another wave would toss it around. The ship would tumble and roll for miles, spilling its entrails all along the way. And it's a big ocean out there.

"We knew from documents that the rest of the fleet made it back to Havana harbor. After the hurricane they sent out scout boats and found the *Atocha* with just the tip of her mizzenmast sticking out of the water. Five survivors were hanging on to a spar, kept alive those five days and nights by a cabin boy who was very agile. They held still and when a seagull landed on one of their heads, this boy snatched it for food.

"Salvaging treasure in 1622 was almost impossible. They used divers who held their breaths. Only about half the booty was recovered. I decided, three hundred and sixty years later, to find the other half.

"I went to Spain's Archives of the Indies in Seville with Dr. Eugene Lyon to determine where to look. The maps pointed to the Matecumbe (Marquesas) Keys. I spent two years dragging a thirty-thousand-dollar magnometer over a hundred and twenty thousand nautical miles. It was a giant puzzle, looking for the *Atocha*. Between storms and over the years I tried to piece it together. In June of 1971 we found an anchor. That led us to the rest of the *Atocha*, lying on a fifty-foot sandy bottom, ten miles west of the Marquesas Keys and forty miles west of Key West.

"From the *Atocha* we found gold coins, silver artifacts, two hundred gold bars, one thousand silver bars, one hundred fifty thousand silver coins, three thousand emeralds, and emerald and gold jewelry. This was the largest treasure recovery of all times. Pieces of eight look like crude silver dollars irregularly shaped. On one side is a cross of Jerusalem with the Spanish version of the Ten Commandments, used to teach the Indians. On the other side of the coins were marks representing other nations the Conquistadors plundered, cutting off heads, fingers, and ears as they looted their way through the land.

"One artifact recovered from the *Atocha* is a poison cup used by the bishop of Peru to test his brandy for Mickey Finns. There were twenty five-carat emeralds mounted inside the cup and a bezoar stone in its center, hinged on a pedestal. If the bezoar turned a darker shade of green than the surrounding emeralds, the bishop refused to drink the brandy.

"This cup is on display in my museum in Key West that I converted from a navy warehouse. Ship timbers were donated to Florida Keys Community College as a cornerstone of their marine archaeology program. This is the first such program in a community college.

"The National Geographic Society filmed the first five years of the *Atocha* expedition in a documentary called 'Treasure.' A second television film appeared on the 'National Geographic Explorer' show.

"Finding the *Atocha* led us to the *Margarita*, which sank in the same storm and foundered on a reef known as the Quicksands. Both galleons have given up lots of treasure so far. The public benefits, because our investors donate the finds to museums and get full tax writeoffs.

"Keeping the treasure was almost as hard as finding it. Admiralty law is complex. When I first brought up a galleon cannon, the state of Florida threw me in jail. I spent more than $1.6 million in legal fees fighting the state, federal government, and S.E.C. I won all one hundred and three hearings. I took my case to the Supreme Court, which ruled 'finders keepers.' I was allowed to keep one hundred percent of the salvage, most of which was found outside United States territorial waters. The owners of the galleons were dead and the government of Spain had to give up claim to the treasure.

"Looking for treasure is nothing new. It goes back at least to the pirates, known a few hundred years ago as 'Brethren of the Coast.'

They did, in fact, hoist skull-and-bones flags and plunder Spain's ships. People were made to walk the plank and there were treasure maps pointing to wrecks. These maps were inaccurate and primitive because of the shifting locations of the wrecks.

"Many pirates were organized by governments to steal treasure from the Spanish who, after all, plundered the Indians. The Dutch had Piet Hind. He had twenty-one ships and twelve hundred men. When the Spanish salvaged half the treasure from the *Margarita*, Hind captured some of the salvagers on their way back to Havana. He took six years' worth of salvaged treasure and left for Holland. He had the sense to split his ships into several groups, each of which sailed in different directions.

"One of Hind's pirate ships went down in a storm off Freeport with some of the *Margarita*'s coins on it. I know this because I salvaged some of them myself. Other ships of Hind's reached Holland and loaded their bounty on traders, bound for the Dutch East Indies where they traded for jewels and ivory. One of these traders sunk in a monsoon and blew onto the coast of Australia. A friend of mine found several chests full of *Margarita*'s coins there!

"In 1983 I found a pirate ship off Cape Cod and salvaged twenty-five hundred coins. I've also salvaged slavers. We found the ship's bell of the *Henrietta Marie*. It was an English merchant slaver that sank in 1699, fifty miles due west of Key West. From research archives I learned she was coming back with slaves and ivory taken from the coast of Morocco. She offloaded the slaves in Jamaica and hit New Ground Reef on the way to New Orleans. That's where we found her, surrounded by leg and arm irons, handcuffs, and ivory tusks.

"I've also found bones. Not just human bones but bones from rats, reindeer, steers, chickens, and pigs. The Spanish boarded animals to have fresh meat at sea. If the chickens laid eggs you had fried eggs. If not you had fried chickens. They also grew vegetables and took on casks of lime juice to fight scurvy.

"I've come across some unexpected findings. We have to be careful when we drag off the Boca Chica navy base. There's a field of fifteen hundred mines on the ocean floor. Detection devices allow us to differentiate between mines and bars of silver and gold. These mines were scattered around the wreck of the *Atocha*. We've also dragged up anomalies: Volkswagens, refrigerators, and a steam locomotive that Flagler was barging in for his railway. Out by Boca Grande we found a Navy Avenger fighter plane. It helped start the Bermuda Triangle myths. I should dredge it up and put it in my front yard someday. I've also found Civil War shipwrecks and modern shrimp boats.

"My greatest find, of course, remains the *Atocha* and *Margarita*. But I'm still hooked on treasure hunting. I'll probably continue to look for more history the rest of my life."

—Interview by William Pohl

Cida Menucelli Bennett

RAISED IN BRAZIL TO MARRY WELL and bear children, Cida Menucelli Bennett was a bride at the age of sixteen, and at eighteen was disowned by her father when the marriage failed. Though her schooling had made her a refined lady, it had provided her with few marketable skills. After several years of varying degrees of success in Brazil, she came to Florida, eventually turning her early training in taste and style into the basis for an improbable business triumph. She now runs one of the few resale clothing shops in the world where a customer may sometimes arrive driving a Rolls Royce. Though her shop, Cida's New for You, stocks many items costing as little as fifteen dollars, it also carries clothes that sell for hundreds and in some cases more than a thousand dollars. Her racks contain fashions by such designers as Ungaro, Lacroix, Chanel, Valentino, and Saint Laurent. The shop's decor reflects her preference for elegance in the French style. Her success has made her a sought-after speaker at national conventions of consignment shop owners, where she conducts clinics on promotion and merchandising.

Because modern immigration from Latin America to Florida is so often connected in the media with drug problems, it is easy to for-

Photo by Henry Rowland

get that most of those who come here are like Cida Bennett, hard-working and deeply grateful for the honest opportunities the state provides. Her unabashed patriotism (she wore red, white, and blue when she received her citizenship) is sometimes mildly embarrassing to blasé native-born Americans, and she is quick to point out that they have no idea how lucky they are. In telling of the years she worked as a maid to gain permanent residence, she is frank about the hardships she underwent but dismisses them as the price of admission to the greatest country on earth. Her final words on the subject are "God Bless America."

"I THINK EVERYTHING STARTED because my family is Italian. You know that in Italian families the man, the boy, is the main part of that family. My brother always have everything and I have nothing, because I'm the girl. I went to school to learn to embroider, and my brother stayed home and have everything my father could give him, and when my brother decide to go into medical school, that was a big thing for my father, of course, who had no instruction at all—just a poor immigrant to Brazil. When he came to São Bernardo, my father had nothing, but he was a good worker and he start as a cab driver, and then he bought his own car and then he had another cab and chauffeur, and it kept adding up. So my father had a little bit of money with sacrifice, and when my brother went to medical school, my father was so excited, so happy, that when my brother was in the fourth year of medicine with two more to go, plus two more in his specialization, my father sold everything he had and built my brother a hospital! It's not a big hospital, but it's a hospital with two floors. God! Today, my brother is a plastic surgeon, still in his own hospital.

"As the daughter, I was raised to be a good mother and house-wife. You know Italian families, they are very serious about who the daughter marries, preferably an Italian. That's what happened. I was married when I was almost sixteen, and he was nineteen. It couldn't last long. I was divorced at eighteen. When the divorce came, my father was terribly upset, because in his eyes it was a good marriage. My husband was Italian and he was wealthy. But my husband left me. He was in love with somebody else, you know. That happens. I wanted to go back to my parents' house, but my father said, 'Oh no! Once married, always married. It's all right for husbands to have affairs. The wife must forgive. Daughter of mine that doesn't live with the husband is good for nothing. I don't want you here!' He never forgive me.

"My father won't talk to me even until today. I just came back from Brazil. I went to visit my father because he's sick, and when I tried to hug him, I couldn't get close to him. It hurts so much. I think the only day that I'm going to be able to hold my father is when he's dead. Then he won't push me away.

"So, I just went to look for a job. And all of a sudden, I went from the wealthy life I had—one week before, I was in the conservatory studying the piano—to working as a maid, because it was the only thing I could do, cook and clean! I felt very depressed. About one year later I found a place as a flight attendant for a company called Cruzeiro do Sul, Southern Cross. I had the tests, and I was approved, so I moved to Rio. It was a little bit better, but it didn't pay too much— I couldn't really afford an apartment in Rio. It was so expensive. At first, I had to live in small little places and share, but as time went by things got better. After seven years, I was living in a beautiful apartment on Copacabana Beach, but that came to an end when I was in a crash.

"The pilot had to make an emergency landing, and when we were landing we had what is called here 'wind shear.' The wind brought the plane to one side where there were sand dunes, and the landing gear was down. When we hit the dunes, that whole landing gear turned upside down and came inside the cabin and brought all those seats to the back with the people in them.

"I don't remember much. Some people were screaming—I think *I* was screaming, 'Please do not have matches on!' 'Cause I was concerned about the gasoline, that it was going to explode and kill us all. They tell me I was not screaming. I don't remember; I was in and out. There was a lady, her son was the governor of that state, and somebody was trying to get her out, but she couldn't go through the window. She was too fat. I remember it was raining and dark and I heard a dog barking, and I was saying to myself, 'Oh my God, I just escaped from an accident and now comes a dog and bites me! What am I going to do with this dog?'

"Because of that I'm retired today. You had to go through medical tests and psychological tests every six months. I don't think I had psychological—conditions, do you say?—good enough to go back to flying after that accident. I still get a little retirement from that, monthly. If you transport it to dollars today, it comes to about thirty dollars. About three years ago I gave power of attorney to another ex-flight attendant so she could receive that money. She's still in Brazil and needed a little help.

"So, after the accident I was back to looking for work, but by that time I was already in my thirties. And at thirty years old, especially in my country at that time (maybe changed now, I don't know), it's not easy to find a job. I tried to do many things but nothing turned out well. And then a girlfriend of mine in Rio told me that her brother-in-law was doing some work for a gentleman that lived in Orlando. When that man came to Brazil, he wanted to get a maid, because he had the idea that women here were from the Amazon, and they work hard! My girlfriend said, 'Listen, Cida. There is an opportunity for you to be in America. At least it's a first step. It's one foot there. Would you like to go as a maid?'

"I said, 'Oh, my God! A maid again! Life has its ups and downs, but I'd do anything to be in America. Anything.' God! To me America was everything one can imagine. Anytime you go out of the country and you say, 'I'm American,' people start looking at you! Maybe you don't understand because you are an American. 'American' means work! 'American' means money! 'American' means anything and everything you can imagine for yourself. And a freedom that we cannot be having in those other countries. Everything wonderful is here. And I said, 'Of course, America! I'm going right now!'

"To tell you the truth, I was so certain that I was going to stay that I sold everything I had. That amounted to a thousand dollars! That was not much. So I left Rio de Janeiro on Mardi Gras Day. There was thousands and thousands of people in costume walking around. All of a sudden, I arrived here in Orlando and the first thing I saw was going through a field with cows! That was quite a difference to me, so quiet. I had left my country, my friends, my way of life. My employer was newly rich and his family were country people from Ohio or somewhere. When I came to work as a maid and live in his house, we had so many of his family and friends come and look at me, just staring at me like I was a rare animal from the Amazon or something. I only knew enough English to give instructions as a flight attendant, so I couldn't express myself. I didn't know what to say or where to go. Part of my job was to cook, and I had to carry a big thick Portuguese-English dictionary to the supermarket! It would take me two hours to decide what was what. I was very depressed.

"On my own time, I was too scared to go out of the house. First, because my boss had picked out an old car for me to buy (that was fifty dollars a month deduction from my salary of two hundred until I had paid five hundred dollars), and the car would break on every corner! Second, I didn't have a day off! Later on, he would give me Wednesdays off, but I would usually stay home and study English, listen to talk shows on radio and try to understand them. I had my mind set to learn English and to get out of there as soon as I could. Many times I went to bed crying, but I never thought about leaving. This was a first step. I knew I was not going to be a maid forever.

"On the day I got my green card, I cried so much. I had left my job as a maid just a little before that, and I went to live in a room in the apartment of an older lady. The first thing she said to me was 'This is my lovely apartment and I want a lovely person to live in here. But no boyfriends!' And I liked that. I think Mrs. Reed was my first friend in America. Then I found a job at the Harley Hotel as a waitress. I thought, 'This is a little step up: I'm not cleaning toilets anymore.'

"So I was working over there and one of the waitresses said, 'Listen, Cida. You should meet Mr. Bennett. He's a very nice man that lives in the hotel, and I think he's wealthy.' When I saw Mr. Bennett, I think he looks cute! And I said, 'Why not?' Here I am after Mr. Bennett, but Mr. Bennett had just left his wife and moved to the hotel, and he didn't want anything to do with any woman at all! It took some time until Mr. Bennett agree, and we married after three months. We have been happily married for twelve years. Very happy. For a while I helped him in his insurance business (he turned out not to be wealthy), but I was not happy being a secretary. I wanted to do something. We can do anything we want in America! So my husband said to me, 'I'm going to help you with five thousand dollars. What do you want to do with five thousand dollars? Do you want to put a down payment on a little house? Or would you like to start a little business?' Well, for five thousand dollars, you can't get much of a house. I thought, 'Maybe if I have a business, tomorrow I will have enough money to buy a much nicer house.' But that's not much to start a business either.

"So I thought back to when I was a maid, and I had gained some weight (everybody does in America—good food) and I could not afford to buy bigger clothes. And then I found out about garage sale (because there is none in Brazil) so I used to buy my clothes at garage sales and in the thrift shop. I used to buy in the bad ones! Full of clothes smelling and—oh, that was awful, but it was the only way I could afford. And I would think to myself, 'Gee, it would be great to have money. I'd do one like an elegant shop in Europe. Very French-style.' And I'd dream about it. So, with five thousand dollars, I decided to try.

"My husband, being in the insurance business, he knows a lot of addresses. On Friday, we would buy the paper, and he would mark the better addresses and make like a route: number one, number two, number three, maybe fourteen in one day. Then we would get up six o'clock on Saturday morning, have breakfast, and go right fast to the first place and be standing right in front of the garage door, waiting for them to open. And I would buy only the things I would like for myself. I would say to myself, 'If I was fat, I would buy this.' We had an old station wagon, an *old* one! And I would put everything in the station wagon and take it home that night and wash, iron, spray a little cheap perfume that I had to make it smell nice, because I remembered how things smelled when I used to buy them secondhand. So I say, *I'm* gonna make them nice.

"I rented a little shop in the Ranch Mall in Winter Park and the rent was three hundred a month. I couldn't afford it, so I got my husband to move his business in there and we put up a nice wall and I rented him that space. That way I could afford the rent on my shop. At the end of three months I broke even, and I put my husband out. I rented the shop next door and we made a place for him there, and then I moved into that shop too. After the third move, he gave up and went someplace else, but not too far away. Now, I have seven shops in the mall. Americans know what's good and they are used to what's good. If you give them what they like, you don't need to pay to advertise, because they will share with their friends, and that's what happened. I never advertise, and I got so many write-ups free. It works; *you* are here! See?

"I don't go to garage sales anymore, now I go to Palm Beach! And I don't drive anymore in an old station wagon, I have a Jaguar and a Mercedes. Palm Beach excites me so much! Every Thursday, I wake up at five o'clock and drive three hours to Palm Beach. And all of a sudden I'm inside those beautiful, wonderful mansions. I've never been in their living rooms, because I'm not a guest, but I go to their closets! Here I am in their sitting rooms, right inside the closets!

"You look at their homes and you never believed there could be such opulence. I was there last week in one of those mansions, and the house is entirely in wonderful white marble, full of sculptures, and right down on the waterway she has a sailboat, and I hear she has a wonderful tennis court and two pools, and the lady talks to me like she was just a lady next door.

"But there is one situation in Palm Beach that's very interesting, because this lady, I don't know her and she doesn't know me. She lives in a penthouse, right on the ocean. And she has a Rolls Royce. I drive my car right up to the front of the building and let her know that I'm here, and she sends down her butler. Her butler comes outside and sign me to go to the garage, and I park my car right next to her Rolls Royce. Then he opens the trunk of the Rolls Royce and put her clothes from her trunk to my Mercedes. He is very nice—has a little striped jacket. I think he is an English. He doesn't talk too much, but says, 'Okay, Cida, this is it.' He calls me by my first name, but who cares?

"As soon as I come back to the shop, I list everything in the computer, with the prices. And I send to her a copy and I put on the side, 'For your approval. Please call collect,' and she never does. She always happy. But I don't know her. The other clients I know, and we agree upon a price. This business, unfortunately, is still not seen too well. There is still a little bit of a taboo about consignment shops. Now, we are breaking through that wall by saying, 'Hey, I'm a business person, too. I'm honest and I can give you very good deals on clothes. Please respect me. I'm somebody. I'm American, like you!'

"I think we've passed that point, really. I'm so honest that when ladies are bringing me some clothes, we are going to talk about the price and put it right on the list of items. Some shops, they give you a list, but they don't give you the prices! Whatever they decide to give you is what you get. You come to my shop, and I turn the computer to you and show you what's sold and how much. The computer makes the checks, telling what item number was sold and for how much. So people know that this is not a fly-by-night business. We work strictly on fifty-fifty basis. If a dress sells for fourteen hundred, that's seven hundred for me and seven hundred for the client.

"None of my clients are listed by their names, only by a number. Absolutely confidential. We do everything in a very secret way because many of them are very well-known ladies. You'd be surprised. At least five of them are nationally known. And there are many ladies right here in town who would not appreciate if I tell other people who they are. That's why I have my own office away from the main store. In the majority of consignment shops, they take their clothes in the shop. I like a little more private for my ladies, where I can offer them a glass of French wine or some coffee while we decide the prices.

"My prices are high for consignment, for used clothes. I know that, but I'm catering for better and better customers. I have people that stop by here, like last Saturday, a lady stopped with a Rolls Royce. And she went inside. And the girl at the counter said, 'Oh, Cida, there's a Rolls Royce outside. She must be bringing a lot of nice clothes!' And the lady turned around and said, 'I'm not bringing clothes, I'm buying clothes. That car is mine.' This is the kind of people that come in, not because they need to buy. They're smart. They like the thrill of coming to a shop and buy an Ungaro dress that cost four thousand dollars for five hundred dollars.

"My husband is American from New York. Sometimes I get a little mad at him. When I want to do something, sometimes he says, 'No, you cannot do that. That's difficult. That's impossible.' I say, 'Don't tell me that. There is no such thing in this country as impossible.' You find a way! You do it! Look at me. I came to America and started making two hundred dollars a month as a maid. Wearing clothes from thrift shops. Buying dirty clothes sometimes. Last year my business closed with five hundred thousand gross. This year we are having an increase of almost twenty percent. I don't mind to say, because I'm paying taxes for that. So, isn't this great?

"And it all happened here. I'm attached to Florida. I think that Winter Park is the quaintest little town. It reminds me of Europe. I have roots here. The best thing is when I fly out of the country, and I come back to Orlando Airport and come through the customs immigration, and there is a line that says, Out of the Country Visitors, and the other says, U.S. Citizens. And you won't believe it, every time I go to that line, I look like a peacock! I say, 'Hey! I'm American,' and I give them my passport, and they always look at it, and then they say, 'Welcome back home.' That puts all the trouble I've had behind. I'm very proud."

—*Interview by John Ames*

Photo by Henry Rowland

CEDAR KEY

Marcia Rogers

JUST SOUTH OF WHERE the Suwannee River spills into the sea, Route 24 traverses slash pines, a low Gulf hammock, cattle ranches, and four bridges that span the bayous. At road's end a small jewel-like island called Cedar Key has claimed a few miles of sand and turf from the shimmering gray waters of the Gulf of Mexico.

The island's remoteness belies a rich history and, later, a spectacular decline. In the very early days, it was shelter to a tribe of aboriginal people whose skeletal remains demonstrate that some grew to over seven feet in height.

Pirates, christened by locals "Brethren of the Coast," frequented the island's hidden inlets, as evidenced by the remains of their shipwrecks. Legends persist that a trove of Bluebeard's treasure lies buried amid the sandbars.

The island's economy took off in the 1840s when shipbuilders and fishers of mullet, oysters, crabs, and scallops moved in. In 1861, the economy was further boosted when the island was connected to Fernandina by a railroad. It is difficult to believe today, but the town of Cedar Key soon became Florida's second largest.

Within decades, however, most of the mullet and oysters were

Photo by Walter Michot

fished out, local shipbuilding went into decline, and a magnificent cedar forest was leveled by a company that manufactured wooden pencils. During the Civil War, the railroad was destroyed by the Union Army and never rebuilt. A small brush and broomstick industry grew as islanders took advantage of a rich stand of saw palmettos, but the invention of plastics eventually led to its demise. As a final blow, the island was devastated by a hurricane in 1896 that swept through, turned tail, and returned to finish the job.

Cedar Key never fully recovered. Today it is one of the few remaining places in the state that retains traces of a slow-paced, rural southern identity. There is a simple fishing pier which harbors some pelicans, and streets of ramshackle bungalows covered with oleander. Only slowly are signs of the tourist trade appearing as a sparse selection of curio shops, restaurants, and condos take root.

The most prominent survivor from Cedar Key's more grandiose era is the Island Hotel. This elegant antebellum building has survived intact with raised verandas and thick tabby walls. Inside, fans hang suspended from the ceilings, potted plants grace a lobby appointed with Victorian antiques, and sunshine filters in through curtained French doors. The hotel's saloons house dark heartwood molding. In one of them a mural depicts island life in the 1930s. It's waterstained, a visible reminder of a hurricane the grande dame weathered.

Marcia Rogers left Vermont in 1980 to find her place in the sun. She eventually stumbled upon Cedar Key and fell in love with the old, dilapidated hotel. She purchased it on April Fool's Day.

"It was an act of faith," says Rogers, a pet parrot perched on her shoulder. "Or folly." She compares herself to a New York City expatriate, written about by Herman Wouk in *Don't Stop The Carnival*, who buys an aging hotel in the tropics. The challenges that Rogers faced included basement floods, mold and rot, financing, a leaky roof, barroom brawls, and a picket fence left unfinished when workmen on the job were discovered to be undercover narcotic agents and chased from town by local shrimpers.

"I never expected making this hotel work would be easy," says Rogers. A decade later, she has put the place up for sale after pouring heart, soul, and money into restoration.

"I CAME FROM VERMONT to find my place in the sun. I needed the warmth and came here looking to buy an old inn on an island. I've always been drawn to islands and their magic ever since I met the Hermit of Washington Island in Wisconsin. He was a man at peace with himself. Like many islands, people who live on them have mystique. They're different.

"I was prejudiced against Florida. I visited my parents in North Palm Beach and saw how far out of balance with nature it was with its condos and cement. It's depressing.

"I decided to look on the west coast of Florida. Route 19 was also developed until I reached Route 24 and the concrete gradually gave way to farmland, pine woods, and marshes. By the time I crossed Number Four Bridge my stomach was in butterflies. I had found, in Cedar Key, something special that hadn't been ruined. It was beautiful.

"I pulled up in front of the Island Hotel in this tiny village and something told me, 'This is the place.' It was for sale. I came running into this rundown, smelly building. The French doors were boarded up and it was seedy but I could see that just beyond the surfaces it had definite charm.

"I stayed in Cedar Key six weeks with a friend of mine who lived in a cottage called Windswept. An omen happened. I woke up one morning full of resolve to buy the hotel. I opened the back door of Windswept and looked out on a gray, overcast day. All of a sudden a hole opened in the clouds and a rainbow appeared. It held for just a minute and then closed. Nobody saw the sun again the rest of that day. I knew then I would buy it.

"My last night in Cedar Key was real cold. It was February and I decided to stay in the hotel. There was no heat so I rounded up a blanket and got into a very cold bed. Suddenly I was warm. Really warm. I felt around the bed and it was like an electric blanket had been turned on. It was eerie. Impossible. But I went to sleep with an incredible feeling of well-being. I named that room the Visionary Room and on April Fool's Day in 1980 I bought the Island Hotel.

"The hotel has a long history. It has been the power point on this island. The building was erected in 1849. During the Civil War the deed was destroyed by Union soldiers and years later this Yankee can't find out the full history of the building.

"During the Civil War this place was a general store and a rooming house above. The owners were not in sympathy with the Union and left. The building served as a barracks for both sides.

"The place became a hotel in 1915. In those early days, it was owned by an absentee landlord from New York City. It was Prohibition and the manager running the place allowed a whiskey still to be built, hidden in the annex between a hip roof and, above it, a second gable roof. I thought this was a legend, but a few years ago when I was doing repairs, I discovered that there were, in fact, two roofs.

"The building has a lot of heartwood and cedar and the walls are twelve inches thick and made of tabby, a mortar mix of limestone and oyster shells. As the oyster shells calcify the walls strengthen.

"This is a fine example of Jamaican architecture. In the center of the building on the second floor is a wind chimney with a vent on top. When the cover-door is pulled open by a drawstring, convection is created and currents are sucked in through opened French doors on opposite sides of the floor. It cools the entire building. It's a wonderful, natural design for the tropics that people in this age of air-conditioning have forgotten.

"The Island Hotel had its ups and downs. It's been through several hurricanes. In 1950 part of the roof was blown away when a heavy-duty storm hit, turned around and came back for seconds, sweeping through Cedar Key again. The owner's solution to flooding was to drill holes in the floors. You can still see water stains in the ceilings, on murals depicting life here in the 1930s and downstairs on a mural, ironically, of King Neptune. We don't have money to restore them.

"The golden era was when Bessie Gibbs and Gibby, her husband, bought the hotel in 1946. They fixed it up and made it work. She was one of the great island characters. Bessie claimed that she used to be a showgirl at the Coconut Grove nightclub in Boston. She didn't show up the night the club burned down, killing hundreds of people trapped inside.

"There was lots of laughter when Bessie came to Cedar Key. She fixed the bar up and used to can-can on the bar with no underpants beneath her skirt. Some nights she danced through the streets in her nightgown. Lots of folks loved her.

"Bessie became mayor. Once she was stopped by a local cop for speeding. When he saw who she was, he said, 'Gee, Bessie, I'm sorry.'

Bessie boomed out, 'What do you mean, you're sorry? I fine myself ten dollars.' You see, she was also the town judge.

"Bessie used to have monkeys caged in the courtyard and a filthy-mouthed parrot on the porch that swore at people as they strolled down the main street. Out in back she had a greenhouse, and in the courtyard a dove cove, a flower garden, and a monkey puzzle tree. She was known for miles around for her turtle soup.

"The irony in Bessie's life was her death. She had missed the fire at the Coconut Grove and lived in fear of flames. Toward the end of her life she injured her back and was confined to a wheelchair. The hotel passed hands. She perished in a fire at her home. It was tragic.

"When I bought the hotel it seemed there hadn't been any mainte-nance or money put into it for fifty years. The roof leaked so badly I created a garden of potted plants, under the leaks, and I had to close off three of the ten guest rooms. Because I needed the money, I'd rent rooms out on sunny days and hope it didn't rain. I eventually earned the eight thousand dollars needed to repair the roof.

"I furnished the place with antiques and 'old attic' that I brought from Vermont. All of Bessie's furnishings were sold at terrible white-elephant sales except for a clawfooted bathtub that remained up-stairs. I brought down carved cherrywood beds, hammocks for the porch, a cracker barrel, and old chests. In 1984 the hotel was placed on the National Register of Historic Landmarks.

"I restored the dining room and began to renovate the rooms, one by one. I've named each.

"Cynthia's Room is named for my daughter. Cynthia selected the corner room in the back and put her writing desk in there. Writers like Dag Hammarskjold chose that room long ago. There's the Vision-ary Room, and the Richard Boone Room, named for the actor who selected it as his favorite; now Jimmy Buffett stays there. Honeymoon couples usually select that one. There's the Sunshine Room, where Pearl Buck stayed. And the Queen Elizabeth Room. It used to be really funky and had loose floorboards. I bought an old waterstained print of the queen and hung it over the bed.

"The Cypress Room is built from hand-hewn cypress boards. I don't have the money to sand off layers of paint that cover them. Over the bed, the Flamingo Room contains an art deco painting of a pink flamingo.

"My first year here was difficult. This is a small island. It has a life and law unto itself. It's not cool to be a Yankee down in the Deep South. Much less a Yankee woman living alone. Much less a Yankee woman who owns one of the largest businesses on the island. Natives are pleasant to tourists. Tourists come but they also go. They wanted to see if I was here to stay.

"Two weeks after I first started I had three women bartenders. One night, the managing woman came to me and said, 'We've got trouble.' A young man who had once robbed the hotel was in the bar drinking. It wasn't cool, especially since one of my bartenders had testified against him.

"I went to see his father, a shrimper from Louisiana, also in the bar. I knew him. He said he'd leave with his son in five minutes. Nothing happened. I went back and he said belligerently to call the law. In the meantime, these tough shrimpers' wives began to beat up my bartenders.

"I had never seen a fight before, here or anyplace. Violence is absurd and here it was happening in my home. It was dark and this brawl was raging, with women pulling out hair and chairs flying across the room. The Cedar Key law, of course, looked the other way. It's a small island.

"I eventually transformed the bar and made it clear violence would not be tolerated in my home. One good thing was that I had to begin bartending myself. I started to meet the islanders. The locals are wonderful characters. They're individuals and storytellers. Fishermen are self-reliant 'cause they've never worked for anyone else and never will.

"There's a marvelous sense of camaraderie. Everyone's known each other all their lives. They kid around. Each day in the post office or café they greet each other like they haven't seen the other guy in twenty years. But they really are glad to see each other. There's a joy to living here.

"There's another side to the people of Cedar Key. I find prejudice hard to tolerate. To this day there's an unspoken code just as there was in the 1930s here when the Rosewood Massacre happened. It was a classic case of a white woman crying rape, with no cause, and the island men banding together and killing every black person—men, women, children—they could find. Blacks are still not welcome on the island after sundown, according to the locals.

"Education is poor in Florida. There's a lack of environmental consciousness. Vermonters had pride, no billboards, a good bottle deposit law and Green-up Day where people voluntarily cleaned litter from roadsides. Trash in Florida is blatant. I have to police the grounds every day. Tomorrow there'll be more trash.

"I once went out with some local fishermen and watched them set the nets for pompano. They also threw their beer cans overboard like the ocean was a trash barrel. The cabbage palm trees are cut to serve heart-of-palm salad, the recipe created by Bessie. No one is replanting. The trees are disappearing just as the cedars did when the Faber Pencil factory cut them all a century ago. My gourmet natural-food restaurant is the only one that *doesn't* serve that salad.

"When I first came to Cedar Key it was a constant struggle. I needed to get away. I drove inland and ended up at a small town outside Orlando called Cassadaga. It's a community of spiritualists and mediums who live in modest homes by a lake. I stopped at one house and asked the man for a reading. He was incredible.

"The first thing he told me was: 'You have a place inside your body the size of a fist that needs healing. You must pay attention to that.' He talked about spiritual guides that would help me out of my financial troubles. In October, he said, I would creatively solve my problems.

"October came and I learned how to turn some equity into cash. He predicted this.

"That wasn't the end of my experiences with Cassadaga. One day a woman came into the hotel. She took my hands into hers. I could feel a lot of power. She started telling me about my past. She accurately told me about my struggles with the hotel.

"This woman looked into the past. She told me two people had died in the back room by the bar. 'One died violently,' she said. 'One of illness.' She said the vibrations were strong and that the spirits were heavy. She said the building could use a seance but that I wasn't ready for it.

"I had no desire to stir things up. But I was curious and did some checking. I learned from some old-timers that Bessie's husband died of cancer in 1960 in that back room the woman spoke of. A man had been knifed in that room as well, long, long ago.

"Shortly thereafter another woman called. She heard of me and asked if I would perform her wedding ceremony. I'm a notary and am allowed to marry people. I agreed.

"The day she checked in I learned she was a medium and she remarked that spirits were in the hotel. She offered to perform a seance. I told her what the other medium said and that I was afraid. It was all so new to me. I'd never been to a seance before. She was very understanding.

"We had a beautiful wedding ceremony with all her friends gathered around the Jamaican wind chimney, which was obviously a power point for the building. After dinner the bride approached me and asked if I'd like to have the seance. Well, it did seem right.

"We went into Bessie's room. The medium went into a trance and almost immediately made contact with some spirits of people she said had worked in the hotel.

"She said one spirit was nicknamed Chatterbox. This Chatterbox spoke through the medium about things familiar to her when she was alive.

"I never met Bessie but was curious to have her called. I felt her presence in the hotel. The medium said Bessie hadn't 'moved on' and couldn't speak with me directly because her spirit was weak from alcohol abuse. Instead she would speak through the spirit of a deceased friend of hers called Star. Star said Bessie appreciated what I was doing, the light I was bringing in helped strengthen her spirit.

"I asked the medium to call a friend of mine named Frederica who had died suddenly. I had missed her funeral. The medium called her spirit and began to feel this dryness on her arms and face. I became speechless. I had forgotten about that. Frederica had a dry skin condition and was always putting on moisturizing cream. I started to cry. The medium said Frederica was very happy and sent me lots of love.

"Later I learned that Bessie had been friends with a woman named Star, and a woman named Chatterbox had worked at the hotel long ago. It was eerie.

"I recently met a man in my bar who's lived here most of his life. He was looking at me and suddenly said, 'You've broken the spell. You've broken the curse on this place. Nobody's ever made it work before like you. The spell's been lifted.' "

—Interview by William Pohl

Jim Maloney, Jr.

ONE OF FLORIDA'S MOST VISIBLE ATTRACTIONS is the Goodyear blimp *Enterprise*. It winters in Pompano Beach and can be seen most afternoons, floating on waves of wind over Fort Lauderdale or flashing messages at night from an electronic billboard over its gondola.

When it is trimmed with helium, a child can easily lift the 192-foot-long airship, including seven passengers. Among several specially-trained pilots is Jim Maloney, Jr. His father was a blimp pilot, and for a while, his son, Jim Maloney III, served on the ground crew.

"It must run in our blood," says Maloney, Jr. "It's easy to see why. There are few things more enjoyable than touring the country from an airship. It's just us, the gulls, and the clouds. We have ringside seats at football games in the stadiums below, and go on tour throughout the U.S. in the summer. It's a wonderful vantage point from which to see the country."

"JIM MALONEYS AND GOODYEAR BLIMPS run in our family. My father, James C. Maloney, Sr., was a blimp pilot and I always wanted to follow in his footsteps. My son, James C. Maloney III, is a licensed airplane

Photo by Walter Michot

pilot and has worked for Goodyear part-time as ground crew on the blimp.

"My dad was born in Fort Smith, Arkansas, and started working for Goodyear on the blimp crew as a young man in California. He worked his way up to ground crew chief. During World War Two the navy enlisted the Goodyear pilots and crewmen for their experience in lighter-than-air (LTA). My dad received his LTA pilot training while in the navy.

"After the war my dad left the navy to fly a blimp for Honest John, a car dealer in Los Angeles that purchased a surplus navy blimp and advertised his dealership on the side of the blimp.

"Later, when Howard Hughes bought a surplus blimp to advertise 'The Outlaw,' the movie he directed starring Jane Russell, my dad was the pilot in charge of the blimp, named the *Outlaw*. The *Outlaw* had one of the first night signs on it, with a script 'Outlaw' in neon on it. My dad would take me along on some of the flights and I had the opportunity to meet Howard Hughes and Jane Russell. In the late forties, I recall Howard Hughes planned on a high-speed taxi run for his flying boat the *Spruce Goose*. He wanted photographers in the *Outlaw* to photograph the event. I was invited to go along for the ride, and to this day you can see the shadow of the blimp the *Outlaw* on the old newsreels of the famous take-off of the *Spruce Goose*, and I was there.

"After Howard Hughes folded up his airship operation, Dad returned to Goodyear to become a test pilot for the navy airships Goodyear was manufacturing. As a test pilot, he had some exciting stories to tell. The one that I remember most was when the controls of a navy airship were mistakenly crossed. The airship did not have any rudder or elevator control. Dad was told to ditch the airship over Lake Erie. Dad decided that he could safely control the direction of the airship with the engines and the ship's altitude by releasing helium and controlling the ballast. He brought the ship safely back to the airport.

"In 1953 and 1954 Stag Beer leased a blimp. Dad toured through the Midwest for two summers and our family traveled with him. From the eyes of a young man it was very exciting to travel around the country following the blimp.

"I was born in 1942 and can remember being around an airship most of my life. I have always wanted to follow in my father's footsteps and be a blimp pilot. I would ask my Dad, repeatedly, to train me as a blimp pilot since I was old enough to fly in high school and through my college degrees. Goodyear was able to attract pilots with increasingly better qualifications, until I had to get a Ph.D. in electrical engineering and my commercial pilot's license to be the most qualified applicant.

"I worked with Goodyear Aerospace for ten years designing and upgrading the new color advertising sign for the Goodyear blimps. Finally, in 1982, I convinced Goodyear management that I was the most qualified applicant for the open blimp-pilot position. Almost twenty-five years after I first asked for the job I finally started my lighter-than-air training. Flying the Goodyear blimp was what I have always wanted to do. I have been a blimp pilot for Goodyear ever since.

"Blimps and dirigibles are both airships. A blimp is generally thought to be a nonrigid airship; the internal pressure of the lifting gas, helium, maintains the shape of the airship. Dirigibles or zeppelins are generally thought of as rigid airships. They have framed structures with an outer fabric cover. The fabric does not have to be gas-tight because you can enclose the gas in separate cells inside the framework.

"The *Hindenburg*, *Graf Zeppelin*, *Akron*, *Macon*, and *Shenandoah* were dirigibles or zeppelins. Goodyear's *Columbia*, *Enterprise*, *America*, and *Spirit of Akron* are blimps made of neoprene-impregnated polyester fabric—a material as thin as two-ply fabric and as strong as aluminum.

"The shape of the Goodyear blimp is maintained entirely by the internal pressure of the helium lifting gas, aided by the air cells (or ballonets) to compensate for the expansion and contraction of the helium.

"The Goodyear GZ-20A and GZ-22 airships, respectively, are 192 and 205.5 feet long, 59 and 60.2 feet high, 50 and 47 feet wide, and contain 202,700 and 247,800 cubic feet of helium. They are powered by twin Continental six-cylinder engines or twin Allison 250-B17C Turbo-prop engines and they cruise between thirty-five to forty miles per hour and have a top speed of sixty-five miles per hour. One advantage of a blimp is that it can stay aloft for many hours without refueling.

"You can see a Goodyear blimp from several miles away. The Super Skytacular night sign with its blue, green, red, and yellow colors can be read up to a mile away. The night sign is a hundred and five feet long and twenty-four feet high and utilizes more than eighty miles of wire. With a mouse or light pen, a technician 'draws' the animations and message copy on a cathode ray tube, which is then copied to a floppy disk, which is mailed to each airship. The floppy disk is loaded into the airborne computer system and generates the spectacular light shows seen at night around the country. Goodyear limits the messages on the airship to mainly public service messages with a few Goodyear-related messages. The Goodyear blimp has given the company global recognition and is used as the corporate logo. The blimps have been used by whale watchers, the Coast Guard, research scientists, and by global media and television crews covering major sporting and special events!

"Each airship has five pilots assigned to it who share the flying duties as required. Each airship has a public relations representative and sixteen to eighteen ground crew members assigned to it to ground-handle the airship during landings. Each crewman has a work specialty—there are licensed mechanics, technicians, riggers, ground support mechanics, computer specialists, and administrative assistants who are kept busy making sure the airship and equipment are ready to travel anywhere in the country.

"Blimps are a very safe mode of transportation despite the fears from the *Hindenburg* syndrome. In over sixty years of carrying passengers, the Goodyear blimps have not scratched one of the million passengers we've flown. Goodyear has the best safety record in aviation history and intends to keep that safety record intact.

"The Goodyear blimps use helium, a safe nonflammable gas. There is very little pressure in the blimp to maintain its shape, about one inch of water pressure. The pressure is much lower than the pressure required to inflate a small balloon.

"We can ballast the airship close to equilibrium, so that it can float around in the air like a cloud. Helium can pick up about sixty pounds per thousand cubic feet. If you want to carry more weight than the Goodyear airships were designed for, you would have to increase the volume of the envelope of the airship. The Goodyear blimp has an operating altitude ceiling of ten thousand feet. Normally we fly around one thousand to three thousand feet above the ground.

"In the summers the blimps go on tour and visit many cities around the country. As we pass overhead, the teachers let the kids out of class to wave at the blimp and we always wave to them. Children love the blimp and are fascinated by it. Some small children know how to recognize the word *Goodyear* before they know how to spell. Normally, when we fly from one city to the next we plan on traveling about two hundred miles per day until we reach our destination.

"I originally came to Florida with my parents when I was about nine years old. I loved it then and always wanted to return. As the old saying goes, 'Once you have sand in your shoes you will always return.' I brought my family to Florida almost ten years ago; now my two sons, James III and Patrick, have sand in their shoes.

"I finally reached my life's ambition, flying a blimp based in Florida. I cannot think of anything else I would rather be doing than being a blimp pilot for Goodyear."

—Interview by William Pohl

Michele Brennan

MICHELE BRENNAN IS SOMETIMES DESCRIBED as the only woman horse-farm manager in Florida. "I don't know whether I am or not," she says. "There are four hundred farms in this area, but if there's another one, I haven't met her." As she shows visitors around the grounds of Dalur Arabians, a neatly maintained enterprise in the heart of Florida's horse country, she picks up occasional pieces of litter dropped by less fastidious workers and speaks fondly of the horses, referring to them in human terms.

"These guys all get fed in separate pens," she explains. "That way, everybody gets a full meal. Nobody can steal anybody else's." It is soon clear that if horses are not quite as important as people in her estimation, they are certainly not far behind. She attributes much of her quick rise in a male-dominated industry to this intense personal involvement, which drives her to provide an exceptional quality of care. She is also frank in saying that she does not enjoy being told what to do. "I learn really quick, so I don't have to be in that position," she says. "That's another reason I've advanced." After a moment's thought she adds, "And I'm a perfectionist."

Michele Brennan is one of thousands of professionals who are

Photo by Henry Rowland

employed in north central Florida's horse industry. The first farms were established there in the early 1950s, but until Needles, the first Florida-bred to win the Kentucky Derby, was put out to stud in Marion County in 1956, there were fewer than five thoroughbred farms in the area. His prestige brought national attention to the region and in the last thirty years, horse farms of all types have largely replaced the cattle ranches which were previously the primary contributors to the local economy.

In many ways Brennan's job goes on twenty-four hours a day. She lives in a residence on the farm and never leaves without telling the owners how long she will be absent. When a call comes into the farm after closing, it rings on her private line, and she presides at the births of all the farm's foals, most of which occur late at night. When mares are due, she keeps track of their condition through a closed-circuit television hookup between the foaling stalls and her house, so even when watching TV, she occasionally goes back to work simply by switching the channel.

Her talents as a manager and as a trainer of thoroughbreds are widely recognized and she occasionally receives offers of jobs out of state, but she prefers Florida. "Kentucky is beautiful," she says, "but it's cold up there."

"I CAME TO FLORIDA because of *Wild Kingdom*. It was my favorite show, and I would watch it every Sunday back in Vermont. To this day I can remember the Mutual of Omaha insurance number. They had little lines all through it: 800-228-9800. I'll never forget—it's not the number any more, but during those days it was. I wrote to Marlin Perkins, asking him what school I should go to in order to become an animal handler. I always had loved animals. My dad went to Notre Dame and majored in zoology, so he always kept the kids' interest up in animals. He was one of those great guys that would make cages that held together for just a little while, so the animals were always able to get loose. When we were little, we had everything: woodchucks, snakes, frogs, chipmunks, a skunk—everything that you could keep, within reason. So you can see why I wanted to work with animals and why I asked Marlin Perkins for advice. He recommended Santa Fe

Community College in Gainesville, Florida. It has a Biological Parks Program which teaches the care and handling of exotic and domestic animals. And they have a ten-acre zoo right on campus—the whole schmeer. As I toured the campus, I said, 'This is it!'

"I came down at the end of August with my little trunk. Here I am: I've come to Florida and I'm like this little country girl let loose in the big city. To give an idea, I graduated from high school in a class of thirty-six, and that's three towns! Gainesville to me is a city, though to everybody else around here it's not. I came down in what's called shit-kickers—which are lace-up, red-leather work boots—and big old baggy jeans and red flannel shirts. That's the attire up there! I've never been so embarrassed in my whole life. It was like, 'Mom, Dad, send money! I need a whole new wardrobe.'

"My first year in Florida was a real period of adjustment. It was so, so hot! I would take a shower and get all ready to go to school, but by the time I walked a few hundred yards to the bus stop, I'd be dripping wet again. By mid-October, when everybody else was in down jackets, I was still running around in my shirt sleeves. I thought, 'This is great,' but they all said, 'Wait until next winter.' Sure enough, by next fall my blood thinned out, and I was in a warm jacket just as soon as everybody else. Now, I hardly ever think about the heat, I'm so busy. I mean, if there's a tree in the pasture, you can be sure I'll be working under it if I can. You can see I have to work in jeans and I prefer to wear boots in spite of the heat and humidity. I even kind of like it, but I do drink a lot of Gatorade.

"The climate is a real plus for the Florida horse industry. We can train all year round, for instance, and the advantage can be seen even in a detail such as washing down the horses. Up north vacuuming is a big thing, because there's a danger of the horses' catching cold if you wash them when the temperature's low, but we can bathe them practically every day of the year after we bring them in from training. If you look at the horses out in the barn, you'll see that they're just as sleek and nice. I think they have a better attitude, too. I know *I* don't like to go to bed all sweaty.

"When I was in school, I gained an appreciation for how fantastic Florida is. Down here there's just everything! I'm really big on wildlife, and Florida has so much more to offer than Vermont. (My mother is going to kill me when she reads this! Or Dad or some-body!) But it's true. I mean, up there, there's no venomous snakes! I *love* walking through a field knowing that I might come across a venomous snake. Up in Vermont we have birds, but not big birds like down here. Here we've got the white herons, we've got the wood storks, which are the homeliest but the funkiest-looking bird, and the eagles!

"We had a bald eagle at Santa Fe Community College—they get all the animals that the Fish and Game Department confiscates—and this bald eagle had been hit by a car or something. Well, the Fish and Game had kept it in just a regular *cage* cage, and it had torn its wings all up. Any bird of prey has to be put in a cage with burlap around the inside because they get startled real easy, and the burlap helps keep them from seeing out, and if they *do* get scared and hit the fence, it's padded. So they brought this bird to us and we put it in a proper cage. My job was to go in and catch this bird up every day and give it a shot of penicillin. That was a chore! I mean, you should have seen the talons on this bird! And to see this thing slowly come around and get its wings revived was wonderful. Then we went and set it free at Paynes Prairie. That is just something I will never forget, all that time and effort, paying off. I mean, I did the same thing with a little homing pigeon in Vermont, but it wasn't anything like watching that bald eagle fly.

"I guess I just got used to Vermont. Each place has its special set-tings, but Florida is kind of mystical. As part of the zoo program, we went down to the Everglades to study. We'd go along some of the trails at night to study the gators, which is really eerie, because their eyes, when they reflect light, are fire red. I mean they're a red that you've never seen before. And their roars! It was mysterious. We'd have to shut off our flashlights as we walked along the trail and you never knew what was going to go underneath you or what was going to be around you. When you woke up in your tent in the morn-ing, you didn't know what was going to be in there with you! I love something uncontrollable, something you can't explain. I'd go to the Everglades again in a heartbeat!

"Anyway, I finished my courses at Santa Fe. Their placement pro-gram is really high. You can work for Sea World, Disney, different zoos, but my love has always been horses.

"I guess that started as a nine-year-old when my sister got a horse. Her name was Mimi. Come high school days, when my sister was sixteen or seventeen, it was either boy friends or the horse. And she kept having me take care of the horse because she had dates and stuff. So finally one birthday she gave her to me, and it was like the best gift anybody could give me. She was twenty-six years old when I got her, but I wasn't satisfied to have her as just a regular farm horse, I wanted to show her. I'm a very, very competitive person and if there is any way I can get in to compete with anybody, I'll do it. And that's the way I saw this horse. We always got Most Improved, because— my poor horse!—she was so old, and I was asking her to do more than she could do. She had a problem with one lead, which is, when- ever they gallop in a circle, the inside leg is always supposed to lead the outside leg. Well, one direction she couldn't do it—she was get- ting so arthritic! But if she couldn't take the lead, I didn't force her to take the lead. I just worked with what I had. Mimi was . . . well, I just miss her so much to this day. She was so neat.

"I still get involved on a personal basis with horses. I think that's what makes me different as far as a horse trainer or horse person goes. All my horses to me have a name, they're not a number. Like a foal I had recently. Before he was born, I reached into the mare— her name is Emprys—and I could feel one foot, and I could feel the nose, but I couldn't find the other leg. It was bent downwards at the knee. The only way to really fix this is to get the mare to stand up. If the mare stands up, everything falls back down into place and you can grab the leg and bring it forward. I was by myself and it was the wee hours of the morning and I couldn't get the mare to stand up. I tried everything, splashed water on her head, went to whaling on her butt. Finally, I managed to get her up. Now, the trick was to keep her moving while I was working at the rear end of her, so I just kept clicking her along and the foal fell back in, and I got a-hold of the other leg just in time, because she laid back down again.

"After that everything went fine with the birth, but unfortunately a situation like that can cause a lot of stress on a foaling foal. Even though they're not out in the world yet, they know that they want to go forward and you're trying to push them back. Because of this, they sometimes get what's called 'neonatal syndrome,' which is what happened to this one. Unfortunately, he got more problems than that because, when he first started to stand (foals try to stand within twenty to thirty minutes of foaling), on one of his tries to get up, he lost his balance so bad that he went head first into the wall. The next day, he wasn't nursing well, which we think had something to do with the neonatal syndrome. And he had ulcers in his stomach. I was giving him Tagamet every day, which is a regular people-ulcer medication. Later, that same foal started getting seizures, probably from nerve damage when he hit his head. We pulled blood on him and his blood count was normal, which means it was something in his vertebrae and there was nothing anybody could do about it. So, we had a hard time with him from day one, and, you know, I gave everything I had, day in and day out for the time I had him, but it got to a point where I had to be realistic. He had to be put down. When I went out there to hand that foal off to the vet, I had to leave, 'cause I was crying. And the vet just turned to me and said, 'I didn't realize it meant that much to you.' To me, horses will never be just a number, and that's why I think I can give them a particular kind of care.

"As a horse farm manager, I've been tested. I'm young and female and I'm not from the South. Sometimes the help likes to see what they can get away with. Many of them are big men, and they can be intimidating, but I'm one of those people that, well, I can be as much fun as the next guy, but don't push me. Like this afternoon, I had a talk with a young man who is one of these 'I-start-work-at-eight-and-I-stop-work-at-five' types. He has no problem with me letting him go at four or four-thirty when things are done, but if I need him to stay a little bit past five, forget it. And I had a horse that just came in from being trained. Now, you do not put a hot horse in the stall, especially when there's grain and hay in there, 'cause you just create problems with colic and so on. So, I told him he was to walk that horse for a few minutes before putting it in its stall. He said, 'It's five o'clock, isn't it?' I said, 'Yes, it is.' And he said, 'Then *you* walk it.' So I flat-out told him that if he's not gonna walk it, don't bother coming in tomorrow morning.

"That's the whole thing working with animals. There can't be a set time! Sure, you say you're coming at eight and leaving at five, but there're gonna be those days! Heck, like during foaling season. If I could go and say *you're* foaling at two and *you're* foaling at eleven, fine. But you can't do that! They foal when they're ready. I don't want anybody to think I'm the big axe, but there's not one original person here, except the secretary, from when I started. I'm a perfectionist and reliability is a big thing with me.

"I don't ask for anything I'm not ready to give myself, like when I got kicked in the stomach. In Florida, when babies are born, they don't shed out real fast—their baby hair—and they're real, real hot. So, what you do is body-clip 'em, just like you do to a poodle. Everybody else was gone to a show in Buckeye, Ohio, and I had the whole kit and caboodle to take care of. There was just myself and one other girl here to do the job. And we were out trying to catch babies and they hadn't been handled a whole lot because we'd been kinda shorthanded in the barn. So I went out to catch one up, and I just had my hand on its rear end, guiding it around, just touching it, showing that I wasn't gonna hurt it. Well, it wheeled and both hind legs got me right in the stomach—laid me right out.

"The girl who was helping leaned over me and grabbed my arms and said, 'I know it's a stupid question, but are you OK?' At that point, I didn't feel a whole lot of pain. I had the wind knocked outta me and I knew something had happened, but I had started this job and I was gonna finish it. Especially with horses, because the biggest part of the horse's brain is the cerebellum, which is the memory. And that's why with horses you do everything in a routine. You break their routine, it just baffles 'em. So I knew this horse was gonna remember this if I didn't continue. I got the halter on her and continued working.

"I'm one of those people that don't go to the doctor's. I just don't, but by two A.M. the next morning, I was ready. I knew I was hurt. The bad part was I couldn't call in sick. Nobody was here to cover. So, I still went out that morning and fed everybody, climbed the fences like a yin-yang, picked up the fifty-pound feed bags and just went about my business. When the other girl came in at ten o'clock to help me out, I went to the doctor's. Well, I had to spend the whole day. That's why I never want to go again—they are the most unorganized people I ever met! It turned out that I had a broken rib.

"They told me—I had to laugh—that I should have bedrest for the next three days. I go, 'Look, I'm the only one on the farm right now. I can't follow this.' They said, 'You gotta do the best you can. It's your body, and if you're not gonna do it, fine, but this is the only way you're gonna heal.' Well, I tried. One day—I was really hurting—I went through the gates instead of climbing the fences when I fed in the morning. Wendy, the girl who came in to help at ten, said, 'Michele, just wait and feed the outside horses at ten o'clock.' I mean, those guys are on a routine! They're fed at eight. I'm not gonna make 'em wait until ten! But for a day, I went through the gates. I didn't climb anything. When I went back for a checkup, they gave me the same prescription. I said, 'Look, I'm fine.' And by that time I was. I could feel some pressure there but no pain. I guess I could have benefited if I had somebody here to take care of me, and I could baby myself a little bit, but it was just me on this whole farm. There were seventy horses out there depending on me. I couldn't let those guys down.

"My favorite time on the farm is sunrise. Even when I have a day off, I don't sleep in. I just like the morning. It's cool, and all the horses are running and the foals are kicking. You have the Spanish moss hanging from the trees. All the birds are out, and down in the pond, the wood storks are feeding. Florida is such a romantic setting. It's home, now."

—Interview by John Ames

Photo by Henry Rowland

Tony Tarracino

IN A HAVANA, CUBA, saloon in 1822, a deal was cut and the island of Key West was purchased by the United States for $2,000. Since that time, saloons have continued to play a central role in Key West's life and history.

One of the island's most colorful bars is located on Green Street. Built in 1852, it is acknowledged as Florida's oldest. Since then, it has passed through various incarnations as icehouse, morgue, bordello, speakeasy, navy bar, and gay meeting place. It's been known as the Blind Pig, the Silver Slipper, the Duval Club. It was the *original* Sloppy Joe's, moved from Havana. It was written about by Ernest Hemingway. He called it "Freddy's Bar" in *To Have and Have Not*. Today the place goes by the name Captain Tony's Saloon.

Tony Tarracino, who bought the bar for $35,000 in 1963, claims to have gotten an early start in life helping his father make bootleg whiskey in New Jersey. During that time, he fell in love with his eighth-grade teacher. She repulsed his advances, saying, "You belong to the world. Go see it." He took her advice when he was run out of town by some toughs who exposed his extracurricular horse-betting scam.

"I love to gamble," says Tarracino. "If I had a choice between

heaven and Vegas, I'd drop the wings and go to Vegas." In 1948, Tony ended up at the Hialeah racetrack "in a pink Cadillac with a blonde bombshell," where he gambled away his savings. Nearly broke, he sent the blonde back in the car and hitched a ride on a milk truck to Key West, in the middle of a stormy night.

"I loved Conch Town. It was just like the Barbary Coast. Pirates, smugglers, the whole bit," he says. "I wandered into the Duval Club and knocked down a few fifteen-cent beers. Little did I know then that someday, I'd own the place and name it for myself."

In his new-found home, Tarracino first became a deckhand. He saved his money, got a captain's license, and bought a thirty-six-foot charter boat. He grew water-wise. In the 1950s he ran guns and ammunition to Cuban rebels and helped smuggle disillusioned people off the island.

His gun-smuggling activities were romanticized in the B-grade potboiler "Kill Castro," starring Stuart Whitman as Captain Tony. Critics panned the movie, calling it "vile and worthless from all vantage points. The highlight comes when the first mate is eaten by a giant sea turtle."

Tarracino also claims to have conveyed hit men on his boat in unsuccessful attempts to assassinate Cuba's Fidel Castro and Haiti's "Papa Doc" Duvalier. "I never did have no luck with assassinations," he laments.

Captain Tony's Saloon greets visitors with a giant stuffed sea bass hung above the front door. Inside, the place is filled with nautical flotsam and jetsam. Thousands of business cards are tacked to supporting wooden beams. The interior looks as if someone plastered the walls with flypaper and then opened the doors to a hurricane. Whatever blew in, stuck.

The same could be said of many patrons who hang around year after year. They come to hear bands such as the Junkaroos, the Hee Haw band, and Jimmy Buffett singing "Last Mango in Paris," a song he wrote celebrating Tarracino.

Inside the saloon by the pool table is a poster of the famous barkeep. Below his gray-bearded, old-salt face, is a handwritten quote: "All you need in this life is a tremendous ego and a great sex drive. Brains don't mean shit."

A self-proclaimed ladies' man, Tarracino boasts fourteen children from three marriages. He says that every woman he seduced in the room over the bar was allowed to paint a colored stripe on the staircase. He tries out lines like, "When I look into your eyes, I feel guilty." Today, the staircase is like a rainbow.

Captain Tony recently became mayor of Key West. After five unsuccessful campaigns that began in 1967 (with the candidate campaigning door to door in bare feet), he finally beat out a man named Tom Sawyer in 1989 "despite his greater name recognition."

"Running my saloon prepared me for higher office," he rasps, a Lucky Strike dangling from his lips. "People voted for me 'cause they know I'm honest."

Today, the mayor presides over the Key West government by day and works the saloon as a greeter by night.

"I WAS BORN IN 1916 in Elizabeth, New Jersey, and grew up in the streets. I was a scrapper. A survivor. We were a heavy Italian family. Well respected. We knew all the Mob. And they knew us. In fact, some of my uncles were blackmailed. One got shot up under a bridge. I loved the Mafia 'cause they looked after their own. They were beautiful. They only killed each other.

"My father became a bootlegger. He was kind of told to, see. It was suggested we start making alcohol. We lived near the Newark dump. When the wind was blowin' right you could smell the moonshine wafting through the neighborhood.

"I spent the Depression years helping make bathtub gin from prunes, potatoes, whatever was handy. I used to get a dollar twenty-five an hour to put on labels which said, 'Bonded in Canada. Twelve years old.' The labels, in reality, were hot off the press.

"I've always been a gambler. For the action. Not for the money. I never wasted time making money. I could've been a millionaire many times but just wanted to make enough to pay the bills and raise the kids. I've got plenty of both. In fact, I have fourteen children. The youngest is three, the oldest fifty-three.

"I live for the action. I learned to add with a pair of dice. Cheating came naturally. I hustled. I sold cockroach powder and wristwatches with no insides. I played with bent cards.

"But still we were all losers. There are no winners in gambling. If you go to the racetrack and lose, tomorrow you're going back to get even. If you win, you go back to win it bigger the next day. It's a never-never land. But it's the action.

"Remember the movie 'The Sting'? Me and my friends had a sting operation like that. My family used to have an old RCA television. Somehow, in between stations, our TV picked up the Garden State race results. There was no picture but we could hear every word before anyone else in town knew the score. Music to our ears. That's how we beat the local bookies.

"I would station one brother by the TV at home and a friend in a phone booth at the bookie joint. When my brother watching TV learned which horse won, he'd call in and we'd place our bets and win! So much so, we started to run out of bookies.

"Like I said, though, there's really no winners. One day, a bookie says to me, 'Wait a minute, Tony. I think you got it both ways.' He was on to me. He wouldn't pay up. He says, 'Go back and see this guy in Lehman's Bar.' I don't want to mention the name of this guy I was told to see, even though he's dead now. Got bumped off by the Mob but he's got lovely kids, know what I mean?

"So I get me these two college kids for five dollars each and all the beer they can drink. They're my bodyguards. We go to Lehman's Bar that night. I walk into the bar, turn around, and presto, the college kids is gone! I never found out what happened to them. I found myself alone but not for long.

"In come these two hoods. I mean gorillas. They had on Chesterfield overcoats, a sign of the big money in them days. I bought one from the Salvation Army once but the sleeves were too long. So anyway these guys pick me up by the elbows and carry me out to a big black limousine. They drive me to the dump where Newark Airport is today and beat the shit out of me. Broke my jaw and ribs. I had Sullivan heels and wingtip patterns printed on my chest.

"I was messed up bad but had the good sense to play possum. They gave me up for dead and left. Figured the bulldozers would cover me over with trash before anyone would find me. I'd be forgotten . . . like the others.

"After they left, I crawled into the swamp and passed out. Two days later, I came to, really beat. I decided to leave town, go to Florida for reasons of health.

"In 1948 all the high rollers came to Hialeah to bet at Tropical Park. Florida was orange trees and white sandy beaches. Took out your camera at the first coconut tree. I loved it.

"It didn't take me long to lose my money. I had a hundred and ten dollars left. I told my girl to take the money and the car—a real humdinger—and go home.

"She leaves and I drift over to the bus station in Homestead. I had eighteen dollars in my pocket. I notice a sign: 'See Key West. Conch Town.' I never heard of Key West. The guy behind the counter tells me that I just missed the last bus. He suggests that I hitch down on the Land of Sun milk truck. That's what I did.

"I remember a real northeaster was blowin' that night, raw and cold. I got on the milk truck and we never saw lights after leaving Homestead until we hit Tavenier, where we stopped to deliver milk to a little grocery. We had a cup of coffee and then didn't see lights again for another forty miles. On Marathon Key there was just a few Negroes living in some shacks.

"Today that same drive on the Overseas Highway is like a stroll through Coney Island. It's all hamburger stands, billboards, and Ramada Inns.

"Put it this way. In them days, the Florida Keys was called the String of Pearls. In the 1960s they were called the String of Clams. Now they're called the String of Oysters. That's progress for you.

"We reached Key West late that night. I was almost broke, soaked and cold. I went into this bar, the Duval Club. I asked the bartender where a hotel was. She was this big mulatto woman and saw I was in a bad way. She took pity on me. She suggested that, instead of renting a flophouse room, I save my money and rent a car at Mallory Square. So I did. Got me a 1929 Plymouth with no windows and spent the night in that.

"Well, for the first time in my life I found myself alone. I sat in that car, thinking. I got to know me. Most of us, we never stop long enough to get to know ourselves. I was lucky and had one brief, glittering moment of truth. I squared if I was a winner or a loser. I liked who I found in that car. I liked Tony Tarracino.

"I got four hours of sleep when I hear these voices singing in the gale. I remember the song: 'When you're old and feeling blue, / And you don't know what to do, / Remember me, I'm the one who loves you.'

"It was coming from this old warehouse on the docks. I looked in through a hole in the wall. There were these beautiful Conch women, singing as they shelled catches of needle shrimp.

"They saw me and asked if I'd like to work. I started to help. I sang songs back to them they never heard before, like 'One Bright and Shining Light' and 'Your Mother's Eyes.' They loved it and sang back to me. It was beautiful.

"It was beautiful, I say, until the pain got bad. These shrimp have a needle between their eyes. My soft hands got cut and infected. I had to soak them in Clorox afterwards. That's life. Always a mix of love and pain.

"Now in 1948 Key West was just whorehouses, gambling joints, slot machines, and saloons. The blackjack tables were fixed. It was a wide-open military town full of bootleggers, wreckers, and sailors. It was like the Barbary Coast only worse. Key West was a part of the United States, but I guess the people running the place didn't take it that seriously. There was plenty of graft and wheeling and dealing and they was flamboyant about it.

"I remember the law in Old Town. If the Wild West had Judge Roy Bean, Key West had Judge Carroll. Both were laws unto themselves. I recall how four guys from Miami were caught with shorts. Under-sized lobsters. They were fined five hundred dollars by Carroll. They were just about to pay up when in walks Captain Lopez, a Conch friend of the judge. He was also caught with shorts; he fished with a broomstick for a pole.

" 'Hello, Captain Lopez,' says Carroll. 'How's the wife? . . . How's the kids? . . . Case dismissed!'

"These guys from Miami are watching all this and get angry. But that's all they got. They never did beat that case.

"What cleaned the law up—a little—was the local newspaper. It came out with a police blotter column on the front page. It was a gossip column that told who went to jail, who raped who, and who was caught gambling. Everyone read it before they read anything else.

"There were no exceptions to the police blotter. I made it twice for gambling and for being intoxicated. (I used to drink up to a quart of scotch a day back then.) Even the editor of the column put herself in the news for getting caught DWI. If a prominent island doctor made the blotter, they'd misspell his name but everyone knew who they were talking about.

"Old Town is a beautiful mix of people. The Conchs are descendents of Tory settlers who colonized the Bahamas. This used to be considered the westernmost Bahama island and many of the ancestors of these old-timers undid the pegs and mortises of their homes and barged them over here.

"Some call the Conchs clannish. The men wouldn't let their women below what's now Truman Avenue and Whitehead Street. We had our differences, personally. They used to put sand in my gas tank. But the wind blows things around. A lot of them got arrested for gambling and whoring. We all learned to live with each other.

"You can dress Key West up but you can never make a lady out of her with her history. There used to be wreckers here. They'd move the channel markers in the harbor into dangerous waters and then 'salvage' cargos from ships that ran aground. There's bootleggers, rumrunners, and drug traders. We've got 'em all in this town.

"This bar we're in also has history. It's the oldest bar in Florida, I think. The building dates back to 1852. There were no refrigerators so this served as the icehouse. Sailboats would take bananas to Boston and ship ice back as ballast, cut from frozen lakes up north. The icehouse doubled as a morgue. Stiffs were put up on the ice until they could be buried. The doors are wide so horses could wheel the ice blocks in.

"When the battleship *Maine* was blown up during the Spanish American War in 1898, news came from Havana to Key West and was broadcast all over the world from this room by the first wireless telegraph. Some of the *Maine*'s crew are buried here on the island.

"Over time, this place was also a whorehouse, a speakeasy called the Blind Pig, a saloon called the Silver Slipper, and the Duval Club. It also went through a stage when it was called Sloppy Joe's.

"The original Sloppy Joe's Bar was started in 1923 in Havana. It moved to this building in the 1930s when a local Conch bootlegger bought it. Ernest Hemingway used to drink here, not in the Sloppy Joe's located down the street today. I could never cash in on a dead man's name so after I bought the place, I named it for myself.

"Every day a ritual took place here. Hemingway and his buddies would go fishing. The bartender's job was to clear these four bar stools by the time they got back, even if they had to beat the shit out of any unfortunate guy who didn't know enough to move when asked. Hemingway refers to this bar as Freddy's Bar in his book *To Have and Have Not*. He wanted to call it Sloppy Joe's but the local bootleggers didn't want to invite any publicity.

"Hemingway loved this place. He also loved the urinal in the men's room, a trough. He told his drinking buddies—the corner gang—that if anything ever happened to the bar, he wanted the urinal.

"In 1937 Hemingway left to fight in the Spanish Civil War. While he's gone the owner of the bar decides to raise the rent to six dollars. Joe Russell who was renting the place says something like, 'Nobody's going to raise the rent on me!' He got together all the winos, boot-leggers and wreckers and in the middle of the night, they moved the building to an abandoned skating rink across the street. They even took the light fixtures. The urinal was taken down the street to Hem-ingway's house. Today the seventy-odd descendants of his cats drink from it.

"When I bought this bar, it was popular with gays. I met Morgan Bird, the gay owner who was losing his ass because he had been put off-limits by the military and was going out of business. All I knew was twenty-four cans of Budweiser but I picked the place up for thirty-five thousand in 1963. I named it Captain Tony's Saloon.

"By then I was a fishing captain. I started as a deckhand on shrimp boats and worked my way into the business. Before then, the closest I had ever come to sea was crabbing on the mud flats of Barnegat Bay, but I soon got to know the waters off Key West better than any-one else bottom fishing. The wind blows things around, and word spread.

"In the 1950s these mercenaries show up on my doorstep. They wanted to invade Haiti and kill Papa Doc. It never happened 'cause one of them died in an accident with live ammunition. We were put on trial in Miami but I got off. You'd think I learned my lesson but soon after, a guy shows up and pays me ten thousand a trip to haul guns, ammo and radios to Cuba—a seven-hour trip. I made ten or twelve trips over.

"Why did I agree to go? It was for the action. These mercenaries were the most interesting guys I ever met in my life. They talked for hours about how to stick fingers in somebody's eyes, ears, or nose and rip out their brains. They lived to kill. Killing was, for them, very impersonal. I didn't have the killer instinct. I never killed anybody. Well, maybe once. But I wasn't like these guys.

"What made these killers so interesting was that somewhere, somehow, a third of their brains wasn't connected to the rest of the system. A whole person is boring. Just a piece of meat with eyes. But these guys were different. And very well educated. They all read the *New York Times*.

"I remember one guy named Arnie. I called him the Owl. He wore thick glasses that made his eyes look huge. He was the demolitions expert. I used to sit there watchin' him holding these two little wires, squinting. If they ever touched. . . . It was fuckin' absurd. Of course, out of the thirty-seven guys in the group, I'm the only one left alive today. It was exciting.

"You know, this bar is a sanctuary. It's a place where anybody can go. It's a kind of church. You can get mentally involved or be a mental cripple here. You can socialize or stick your head in the ground and leave your ass outside like an ostrich.

"The place holds such memories for me. Here's where I first met Shirley. Shirley. First names are great. Last names don't mean shit unless you're signing a check.

"We drank our scotch and soda here. We played Fascination. We got married. I bought the place. Captain Tony's Saloon soon became one of the greatest gay bars in the world. And I was straight!

"The bar got big. Very big. We had the Junkaroos, a great band. We got written up in all the newspapers like the *New York Times*. Everyone's come through here at one time or another. Sometimes as I'm closing the joint up at three in the morning I can still see Tennessee Williams, sitting on a stool in the twilight, smoke curling from his cigarette. Tennessee hung out here. So did Truman Capote. He used to run into the men's room after the navy boys with his pocketbook, yelling 'Hello dahlings.' I had to rush in after him to prevent them from beating the shit out of him. Robert Frost drank here. Geraldine Page, Elizabeth Taylor, and Al Smith ate their grunts and grits here. Harry Truman came in for bourbon and beer—some mornings. The place was big.

216   Key West

"I became a high roller. Got a credit marker in Vegas for ten thousand dollars. Henny Youngman and Buddy Hackett would invite me to dinner. And I bought my first pair of three-hundred-dollar shoes. I used to be so poor I stuffed my shoes with newspapers. The holes got so big the newspapers fell out. And now three-hundred-dollar shoes and the high life.

"I never wore those shoes. They're still in the closet. And the high roller found himself rushing back to Key West. The Tony Tarracino I found on that cold, lonely night in the Plymouth. The real Tony. The Tony I liked. I put back on my T-shirt, took out the trash, and I was happy again. People have offered me millions for this place. I can't sell it. Ever. It's become a part of my soul.

"See these wrinkles on my face? They're not wrinkles. They're scars. I'm gearing up for my last fight. Key West is the southernmost place in the United States. It's just ninety miles from Cuba and lies at the same latitude as Cairo, Egypt. Over the years a beautiful ritual has developed on the docks at Mallory Square. Each night at dusk people come to the docks to bid goodbye to the sun. They play flutes, sing and dance. They wait for the sun to go down in silent reverence. It's a beautiful happening.

"Developers in this town want to stop it. They want to fence off Mallory Square and kick out the vendors and street people. They want to charge admission to watch the sun go down. Cashing in on the sun! Such greed. Such a symbol for Florida today!

"I have been asked to fight. People know I'm honest. They know that everything here's getting polluted and developed and built up with condos right up to the edge of Old Town. They know I can expose the developers and defeat them. And I will if push comes to shove.

"You ask if all the greed and pollution and development here bothers me. It does and it doesn't. There's an old Conch expression that says, 'When the wheel comes around, a big hurricane will come along and Key West will go right back to being a fishing village again.'

"You'll see. The wheel's goin' to come around again. And when it does, it'll be beautiful."

—Interview by William Pohl

Photo by Walter Michot